How To Be

A GOOD SECRETARY

*the text of this book is printed
on 100% recycled paper*

How To Be
A GOOD
SECRETARY

by

Marie Lauria

**Instructor, Secretarial Practice, Fordham University
School of General Studies**

▥ BARNES & NOBLE BOOKS

A DIVISION OF HARPER & ROW, PUBLISHERS

New York, Hagerstown, San Francisco, London

FOREWORD

Darrell B. Lucas, Ph. D.

PROFESSOR OF MARKETING

THE SCHOOLS OF BUSINESS

NEW YORK UNIVERSITY

The methods explained in this book have been continually demonstrated by Marie Lauria in her capacity as a secretary for an executive in a large company; also as instructor in secretarial practice in the Fordham University School of General Studies. There can be no better proof of the soundness of the ideas presented here.

How *to Be a Good Secretary* is a book which today's executive will hope his secretary will read and study. Application of its recommended practices can assure maximum efficiency in the daily functions of a busy office. The competent secretary will become increasingly indispensable by adding to the efficiency and output of her executive. From the standpoint of the secretary, the full development of her talents will add to her interest in her job, and to her business progress.

The most unique feature of the book is the remarkable balance between guidance on specific skills and suggestions for broadening the personality. The author makes clear that a mere accumulation of relevant skills is not sufficient; there must also be

5

intellectual and personal growth. This book contains an impressive program for nurturing the kind of development so evident in highly successful secretaries.

Both the beginner and the experienced secretary will find practical value in this volume. It contains all of the essentials the secretary needs at the start, plus important guides for continuing success in her chosen career.

CONTENTS

INTRODUCTION

In our complex business world of computers and new ways of transacting business, the need for a *good* secretary never ceases. The executive finds that as the pressures mount, more and more is expected of him. A great deal of the pressure can be removed by a secretary who can help him complete his day's work.

As a secretary, you are a major communication link between your executive and his associates, the office staff and the public. Because of your important linking position, you can play a vital role in helping to create and maintain a smooth-running business office. For this reason, you need to know all the *short cuts* and *efficient working methods*.

The purpose of this book is to provide you with practical on-the-job training that can be beneficial to you in keeping the business routine moving. The book is especially designed to give you—

- new ideas and techniques;
- an opportunity for personal development;
- ways to develop initiative, adaptability and self-assurance;
- an opportunity to exemplify loyalty and conscientiousness; and
- methods that will increase your value in the business office.

Attention is also focused on: looking ahead; planning; managing time efficiently; assuming responsibility; exercising initiative without being aggessive; handling telephone calls properly; improving your conversation; developing a good memory; effective letter writing; better typing; better transcribing performance.

Because today's accent is on self-improvement and skill-development, this book can be of great value to the girl who is planning a secretarial career, and to the girl currently engaged in secretarial work.

Marie Lauria

How To Be

A GOOD SECRETARY

Chapter 1

IMPORTANT JOB
REQUIREMENTS

Almost anyone pursuing a secretarial career can be a secretary. But will she be recognized as an outstanding success?

One busy executive outlined the essential requirements associated with his activities.

"What I need," he said, "is a secretary who can transcribe her shorthand notes intelligently.

"She must be able to spell.

"She must have a good understanding of grammar and composition.

"She also must have a natural sensitivity to the nature of her position.

"In other words, she must *know her job.*"

The expectations voiced by this employer are re-echoed by many executives of industry, of government agencies, of the professions, and of advertising.

Never before has the need for good secretaries been so great. Employers in almost every field of business are faced with an ever-growing problem of finding *just the right person* to take over the office agenda.

In our complex business world of computers and new ways

of transacting business, the secretary's performance—what she does, and how she does it—is becoming increasingly important.

As a secretary, you should recognize the basic differences between your position and that of a stenographer. The stenographer is expected to take dictation, transcribe her shorthand notes, do statistical typing, filing, answer the telephone, arrange appointments, and occasionally open the mail. The secretary is expected to do all these things *and more*.

In the role as "top-flight" secretary, she performs many of the clerical and managerial tasks that her busy executive may not have the time to perform.

Such duties include:

1. Planning, organizing, and controlling the workload.
2. Being creative on the job.
3. Dealing with emergencies.
4. Gathering facts and presenting them meaningfully.
5. Performing as office manager.
6. Aiding in decision-making.

In addition to being competent, the outstanding secretary should be a warm and understanding individual, whose main purpose is to anticipate the needs of her executive and reduce his workload.

YOUR BASIC SKILLS

Besides having a thorough knowledge of her duties, the secretary should have a sound, broad knowledge of business in general; further, a specific knowledge of the particular business of the company in which she is employed. With such a knowledge she will be able to make decisions and will also be able to advise and help her executive. The more knowledge the secretary has, the more valuable she becomes.

A good education is an essential element in holding a high-level secretarial position. Any weakness in the education of the secretary is quickly perceived in the quality of her performance.

As a secretary to an executive of a company, your basic skills should include the following:

1. SHORTHAND AND TYPEWRITING

These are the foundations of secretarial practice. The more expertly you perform these skills, the more efficiently you will be able to function as a secretary.

In order to improve your shorthand-speed ability, train yourself to take dictation at always greater speed levels. Radio and television news commentators usually speak in varying speeds. Choose those commentators whose speed levels are comfortable for you to take down in shorthand outline.

Below are shorthand speed requirements usually associated with certain fields.

General Business Dictation— 80-120 words per minute
Medical Dictation   — 90-100 words per minute
Legal Dictation   —120-135 words per minute

If you can take 100-120 words per minute, you are prepared to perform at a routine secretarial position. The most exciting secretarial positions, however, are with the dynamic and swift decision makers who necessarily think and speak rapidly. These executives require a secretary whose stenographic ability is above average.

Since shorthand is a language in itself, the highly skilled secretary possesses an extensive shorthand vocabulary built upon a thorough knowledge of shorthand outlines.

2. BUSINESS-LETTER WRITING

The ability to write effectively is an important business asset. Much of today's business is transacted in writing letters and reports. That is why *letters* play a much more important part in business than most secretaries realize.

Because every business message is designed to achieve a specific objective, you should have an acquaintance with the particular interest and, if possible, the emotions of the reader. No business letter is effective unless it retains the reader's good will.

Since your secretarial ability requires you to answer routine inquiries and compose correspondence, further development of these skills is essential if you are to perform more efficiently and expertly in the area of business communications.

3. Accounting (or Bookkeeping)

Record-keeping is an essential business function. As a secretary, a knowledge of bookkeeping, even though it be of the simplest kind, will be useful to you in performing the occasional tasks that involve figures. The amount of knowledge of bookkeeping that is necessary varies with the particular position. The position may be such that the secretary is required to spend a good deal of her time in managing the financial affairs of her employer. In such a case, it would be necessary to have a complete and thorough knowledge of accounting. Such a position, however, is an exception.

Nevertheless, a knowledge of the rudiments of accounting, such as "debit" and "credit" will come in handy if you take charge of your executive's bankbook or checkbook or of his expenses incurred while traveling on company business.

4. Business Machines

The typewriter isn't the only office device which plays an important part in aiding the secretary to turn out a quantity of work with the least amount of effort. Other appliances are also helpful in speeding up production in the business office. Many large corporations are well equipped with special machines that successfully perform a great deal of the routine work of their vast organizations. Some business machines, of course, are so specialized in their operations that only an on-the-job training in handling them will suffice.

As a secretary, you are expected to be acquainted with the operation of some of the more commonly used office machines, such as the following:

Addressing Machines
Adding and Calculating Machines
Bookkeeping and Billing Machines
Duplicating Machines
Dictating Machines

The widespread use of the dictating machine by busy executives makes it necessary for the secretary to be familiar with its operation.

5. FILING

Filing is an important function in most business offices. Every secretary should have a knowledge of the system of filing best suited to meet the needs and demands of her particular office. Whatever system of filing you use, it is important that you carefully and consistently follow it.

Despite the fact that shorthand and typewriting are the indispensable secretarial subjects, no one can overestimate the essential roles English, spelling, and composition play in the day-to-day drama of office work. Today, creative writing talent is the possession of many a secretary and is highly valued by important executives.

Besides English, a knowledge of social studies and one or two languages will be useful in securing a high-level secretarial position. Among foreign languages, Spanish would seem to be of special importance.

SELF-EDUCATION

The difficulty with some secretaries is that they are too often content to be just average rather than the best. If you intend to be a *first-rate* secretary, then you *must* pull yourself up above the ordinary secretaries. Big rewards are only for the secretary who is above average.

Nearly every secretary can easily and quickly learn the fundamentals of secretarial work, but to this knowledge she ought to add those little refinements that will make her work of more value to her employer.

Every little point, therefore, that will aid you in becoming efficient and successful should be seized upon and put to work.

1. Read Good Literature

As a secretary, you cannot ignore the need for grammar in the business office. But, more important, you must also be a well-read person. Your familiarity with good literature will help you to express your own thoughts properly, attractively, and effectively.

Below is suggested reading material that should provide you with enough information to keep you well versed in current topics and important news events.

> *Magazines:* *Business Week*
> *Newsweek*
> *Reader's Digest*
> *U.S. News & World Report*
> *Newspapers:* *The New York Times*
> *The Wall Street Journal*
> (your local newspaper)
> *Books:* Biographies
> History
> Plays
> Travel

Poor or undeveloped reading habits have too often chained secretaries to unimaginative chores. If you possess a strong literary foundation, you will find it a good preparation for more challenging and exciting positions that can be yours. Also, the more you read, the wider your interests will become. As you become better informed about more and more things, you will win respect for your opinions in your daily conversations with your employer and others.

An honest answer to each of these ten questions will help you to determine how well informed you really are:

1. How many newspapers do you read?
2. Do you look at all the pages in the newspaper or do you read only certain parts?
3. Are you a "Headline Reader," "Front Page Reader," or "One Subject Reader"?
4. How many magazines do you read?
5. Do you attempt to analyze the news and all information as you read it?
6. Do you read for: information, recreation, or both?
7. How many radio or television news commentators do you listen to weekly?
8. Do you read biographical, historical, factual or only human interest material?
9. Do you read carefully, so as not to get the wrong impression of the material you read?
10. Do you believe you sincerely get all that you should out of your daily reading in the time available?

2. TAKE ADULT-EDUCATION COURSES

In modern business practice, the need for "specialists" keeps growing. There are many ways in which you can increase your value in the business office. Adult-education courses of varying kinds are available to anyone who is seriously interested in developing himself or herself.

Many institutions of higher education provide courses in such subjects as:

Accounting   Business-Letter Writing
Banking   Computer Programming
Business Law   Contracting

Insurance	Reading
Language	Real Estate
Management	Speech and Voice
Purchasing	Improvement

You may elect to take courses in a subject about which you already have some knowledge and thus work toward developing your skill as an expert. Or, you may take up a new subject which can be usefully applied to business (and social) situations. The increased knowledge will help you develop into a more interesting personality.

The mark of an efficient secretary may be observed in many different ways. What some secretaries fail to realize is that it depends in essence on having self-confidence, dependability, and "know-how."

YOUR PERSONAL QUALIFICATIONS

Your personal qualifications play an essential role in your getting and holding a top-level secretarial position. To get the most out of your career, you will want to possess and develop certain attributes that enable you to stand out among others.

1. ADAPTABILITY

Everyone is endowed by nature with certain abilities and aptitudes. Adaptability is one of your most important attributes and determines how well you are able to perform at your job. Not all secretarial positions are alike. Your manner of performance varies with the organization in which you are employed, the nature of the position, and the particular person for whom you are working. Because employers have different habits and work preferences, it is important at all times to make the best possible use of your ability to adapt while you are secretary.

Also, since new principles and procedures of transacting business are constantly being laid down and followed, the ability to perform your special skills in the various segments of the business routine is a vital asset. As a secretary who possesses diversified talents, you will go far in your career. Today, executives depend a great deal on secretaries who are able to relieve them of numerous details and be "coordinators" in business. Such positions, however, can be attained only by the ability to adapt to change without difficulty so as to conform to new conditions. Some points to remember:

a. Be receptive to new business methods.
b. Show an interest in learning the business.
c. Know why certain jobs are done certain ways.
d. Listen to the experts in your business. You'll be surprised how much you can learn from them.

2. LEVELHEADEDNESS

Levelheadedness means having common sense and sound judgment. Unfortunately, many people suffer from a lack of poise. They fear they'll say or do something wrong. The trouble is that they are substituting emotional thinking for logical thinking. They are so busy planning what they are going to say or do next that they fail to catch what the other person is saying. At a business conference they fear they will seem awkward and won't make a good impression upon their colleagues or their executives. Tension upon being introduced whether socially or in business stems from a feeling of inadequacy. A secretary fears she will do something wrong and will not please her executive.

To function intelligently you must control your emotions. Don't be the kind of secretary who falls to pieces every time you are asked to perform an important rush assignment. This is no time to become hysterical or confused. Remember, your executive is relying upon your secretarial ingenuity; and you can be a great help to him if you can do your part of the job as fast as possible, with the least amount of apparent effort or strain. When you become emotionally upset, you are unable to think clearly. And no matter how hard you try to do a good job, under such conditions, everything that you do seems to be wrong.

Poise is assurance. Observe the poised secretary in your office who devotes her full attention to what she is doing. She is not concerned with herself because she can effectively lose herself in what she is working on. The secret to logical thinking is to remain *calm* and *poised*. True poise rests on knowledge and confidence. It is knowing your job and having faith in yourself to do the right thing. Well aware that you are fully able to master any situation that might arise, you can concentrate on your work. Three simple steps:

    a. Read all assignments carefully before you begin work.
    b. Be sure you understand all the facts.
    c. If anything is not clear to you, ask questions.

These three steps will improve your efficiency, your output, and your usefulness.

3. Being a Self-starter

The ability to be a self-starter is a valuable asset which you, as a secretary, must do your best to acquire. Some secretaries seem to feel that once they obtain a position, they need not employ further skills. This is a mistaken impression. Bosses are ever in search for a secretary who is a self-starter. And as such a secretary, you must constantly prove your worth. Here are some ways to do just that:

    a. Keep thinking of new and better ways to improve your performance.
    b. Work on your own without the need for constant supervision.
    c. Have imagination to plan and look ahead.
    d. Develop your own executive qualities by performing any required task, regardless of how difficult or simple it may seem.

e. Make a special point of handling things efficiently while your executive is away.

There are numerous ways in which you can initiate action; one way is your *willingness to assume responsibility*. When the opportunity comes calling, it usually seeks out the resourceful . . . a person who can take over a given situation and be counted on to perform a task well. Let one of those persons be *you!*

4. BEING A GOOD OBSERVER

When a person is observant, he is usually being perceptive and alert. Alertness is a conscious awareness of everybody and everything. Nowhere is this quality more important than in the business office. If you aspire to reap the benefit of the real joys that can come out of a successful career, begin now, and turn every circumstance to the best advantage.

a. Learn all there is to know about your job and your firm.

b. Observe everything that goes on about you.

c. Read all matters pertaining to the business, except those marked "personal."

d. Show a genuine and sincere interest in everything you do, the little and less important jobs as well as the big, important ones.

e. Show your interest in the welfare and activities of other people.

f. Read as many business periodicals and trade journals as you can in the time you have available. Reading keeps you informed. If you do much well-selected reading, your perspective as well as your horizons will be enlarged.

5. INTUITIVENESS

To be intuitive is knowing or perceiving by intuition. Intuition is instantaneous apprehension—attaining to direct knowledge without conscious efforts. Intuition is not restricted to the clairvoyant; it is part of everyone. Unfortunately, some people never make use of it; others don't ever develop it. The mind's ability to visualize and sense things is a great asset. One way you can exercise intuition in your job is to develop a "feel" for your responsibilities. For example: Perhaps you are asked to read a certain report. Somehow you sense a wrong figure in a tabulated column. In double-checking, you discover an error. To possess an almost uncanny intuition about your responsibilities is, in part, the result of *knowing every phase of your job.*

6. FLEXIBILITY

Flexibility is another asset which enables you to adapt to situations or existing conditions. As already indicated, no two companies operate in precisely the same manner. Each has its own specific rules and regulations. Even departments within large corporations do not all function alike. Whether you are at a new job, or transferred to another department, no matter how experienced you think you are, it is essential that you conform to company or departmental rules and policies and *adapt* yourself to the required methods of performing your duties.

Like large corporations, no two bosses have exactly the same methods of doing things. For a better secretary-boss relationship, be flexible. Learn first, what are your executive's work preferences and determine to go along with him. It becomes a distinct advantage if you adjust your own personality to that of your executive and *adapt* yourself to his individual and particular methods.

7. TACT

Tact is a keen sense of what to say or do in order to maintain good relations with others or to avoid offense. Tactless incidents arise when someone says the wrong thing at the wrong time. Except for a person who is deliberately cruel, no one wants to make tactless remarks and hurt the other person's feelings. Such remarks just seem to slip out. Your ability to meet embarrassing or upsetting situations is evidence of your poise and your concern for others—their thoughts and feelings. Whether you are a natural or merely an occasional offender, here is how you can avoid making social or business blunders.

a. *Be aware of what would be offensive.* Suppose a certain Mr. X, who makes a habit of calling unexpectedly on busy executives, stops in the office. He is polite, friendly and intelligent, but he insists upon making unscheduled office visits, despite the frequent polite dismissals he has received from many efficient secretaries.

To tell Mr. X that Mr. B does not want to see him would be distinctly discourteous. As a secretary, the most tactful excuse to use would be: "I am sorry, Mr. X, but Mr. B is out of town on business. He is expected back in his office some time next week. Perhaps Mr. B may be able to see you then?"

Mr. X does return next week, and Mr. B is still unable to see him. Mr. X can be told tactfully that "Mr. B has been attending meetings all day which resulted from his visit out of town. As much as he would like to see you, it is really impossible today. Would it be convenient for you to come another time?"

Since tact was employed in both instances, Mr. X will surely come back again.

You might ask, "Suppose I run out of excuses if Mr. X insists upon coming again?"

Then Mr. B should take a few minutes from his schedule to talk with Mr. X. Not to see him at all would be discourteous. Chances are that Mr. X wants to discuss one of his products which might be useful to Mr. B at some future time.

b. *Think before you speak.* A nervous habit of speaking too rapidly without thinking of what you intend to say can create offense. For example, on the telephone, you may be asking someone to come to see your boss and in your eagerness to be accommodating, you may say, "Mr. B will be glad if you can come for only a short visit." Actually, what you meant to say was, "Mr. B will be glad if you could come, even if it were for only a short visit," and this is what you should say.

c. *Wait until the other person is ready to hear what you have to say.* Some people are so impatient to discuss their particular topic that they break in on a conversation, without showing consideration for the other person's thoughts. Such a habit is not only rude but most annoying.

d. *Remember little details.* You can overcome absentmindedness by concentrating on everything that people say to you. Remembering a person's name, what he does, where he comes from, even a hobby, if he has one, can be important.

In the business office especially, *tact* is exceedingly important. Practically no situations arise where you do not *have to be tactful.*

Working with your executive—you must show concern for his feelings by being constantly on guard not to offend him.

On the telephone—you must always be courteous to the telephone caller by showing a willingness to be of service.

Regarding your co-workers—you must be able to work with them in harmony so as not to create disagreements.

When visitors come to the office—you must be pleasant and friendly so that the visitor feels he is welcome.

8. FRIENDLINESS AND BEING PLEASANT

A poised individual feels at ease in any group and can get along with others. He possesses a quality of personality that enables him to attract the friendship of others to him. He is bright, happy, cheerful, and sympathetic. He has an encouraging word for everyone. In companies where groups of people spend most of their time working together, being on friendly terms is essential, if an atmosphere of harmony and tranquility is to be maintained. A feud or a personality clash can be disastrous. To be able to command the respect and attention of others, you must *first* learn the art of making people like you. Observe all the codes of office courtesy. Such simple expressions as, "Good morning"; "Good day"; "Please"; "Thank you" are valuable in keeping the good will of your fellow-workers. Above all, learn to accept comments and criticisms graciously. A disagreeable attitude will get you nowhere. An essential requirement for being liked and becoming popular is a *pleasing personality*. Remember the slogan: "Service with a smile"—so start *right now* by being friendly and pleasant. Some of the benefits to be derived are poise and self-confidence, a happier life, and more friends.

9. Accuracy and Thoroughness

In the business office, accuracy and thoroughness are inseparable assets. *Accuracy* is freedom from mistakes or errors. As an efficient secretary, you have the opportunity to exhibit your ability in every phase of your job. This calls for paying strict attention to details.

a. Letters or typewritten work should be neat in appearance, and evenly centered on the page.

b. The body of the letter or the text of other typewritten material should be accurate as to facts, grammar, and punctuation.

c. Dates, figures or sums of money, and spelling also should be correct.

d. Double check everything before you let it leave your desk. A mechanically accurate typewritten letter or report makes its meaning clear both in the wording and in the way it has been typed. Accuracy is essential if your letters or reports are to create a favorable impression on the persons receiving them.

Most busy executives don't have the time to pay attention to details. That is why accuracy must be part of the secretary's initial skills.

Thoroughness is completion in all respects. Concentration and attention to detail are the keys to thoroughness. Focus your mind on your work and be concerned with its completeness. You will find that to do a job well is a splendid satisfaction.

10. Loyalty and Truthfulness

There are numerous ways in which you can be "a perfect helpmate" in the office. Exhibiting *loyalty* is one way. As a secretary, you must have this qualification, for you are in a position of trust and often are called upon to handle executive matters. For this reason the following suggestions are to be followed:

a. Act always in the best interest of your executive or superior.

b. Relieve him of as much work and worry as you possibly can.

c. Carry out *his* wishes, not yours.

d. Keep his personal business to yourself if he has entrusted you with confidences.

e. Anticipate his needs as much as you possibly can.

Being *truthful* is another way you can exhibit your secretarial ability and expertness. Truthfulness means telling the exact truth, especially with regard to the gathering of facts. In many instances, executives depend upon their secretaries for factual information. In such cases, the information you provide must be accurate if your boss is to rely on it. In providing information, gather facts that are accurate, meaningful, and intelligently organized. Pay particular attention to dates and definitions, and copy everything you select exactly as it is presented. Unless your executive can rely on the accuracy of the information you give him, he is at a great disadvantage in carrying on his work. As you advance, you become more than just a taker of letters, a typist, or a receptionist. You become in addition a reliable source of information on which your executive can rely.

11. Forethoughtfulness

Forethought is the thinking out or planning ahead of some future event and taking the necessary prior action to forestall a later one. In the business office unusual or difficult situations constantly arise and forethought on the part of the secretary very often can help to maintain the good image of her company or executive. In thinking of the best interest of your executive, you can exercise forethought in many ways. Here are two instances:

1. Take care of details that your executive may have overlooked. For example, you might send him by Special Delivery an important letter or document which he might have forgotten to take with him on a business trip.

2. Save him from embarassing situations. Suppose your executive, Mr. Brown, has just left the office to keep his luncheon appointment with Mr. Smith at a businessman's club. You receive a telephone call from Mr. Smith, saying he is taking along a friend and would like to know if Mr. Brown approves. Disappointed at learning that he has just missed Mr. Brown, Mr. Smith tells you he has decided, anyway, to take a chance and have his friend join them for lunch. Such a situation could be embarrassing. As an efficient secretary, you will want to resort to some face-saving measure. The most logical thing to do then, is to have Mr. Brown paged at the club to inform him as soon as he gets in that Mr. Smith is bringing along a friend. Knowing in advance what to expect, Mr. Brown is able to handle whatever situation might arise in a diplomatic manner.

With the knowledge of your ability to master any situation that might come up, your executive will rely on your secretarial ingenuity to free him from any and all possibly embarrassing or involving situations.

12. INITIATIVE

Initiative is the power to exercise one's own judgment independently. This is a quality which every secretary should possess and develop. Most executives appreciate a secretary who has the capacity for independent judgment and action. In exercising your own initiative remember that you must always act in the best interests of your executive and your company. To this end you must:

a. Constantly think up new and better ways of helping your executive with his responsibilities.

b. Know where and how you can improve your own efficiency.

c. Develop your executive qualities by persistently carrying out everything that may come within reach of your secretarial duties.

Good judgment and experience are the foundations upon which initiative lies. If you find yourself weak in initiative, you should make every effort to develop it.

The secretary who is most wanted by busy executives is the one who can be left to her own resources, in the confidence that she can be relied upon to make and carry out meaningful plans.

13. Self-confidence

Nearly everyone has a natural tendency to be nervous when confronted with any new and important experience. FEAR induces tension. In many instances, it robs us of our emotional stability. Even some famous personalities in the entertainment world encounter a fear known in the profession as "stage fright." However, through proper training in the early part of their acting careers, many performers have been able to overcome this number one enemy . . . FEAR.

Like the stars in the performing arts, as a secretary, you, too, can learn how to control your emotions. You *must* learn how to develop self-confidence. This will give you poise and self-assurance. More important, it will give you faith in your abilities.

14. BEING A GOOD LISTENER

A very important function for a secretary is *listening*. To listen carefully requires a conscious effort to hear, to heed, or to take advice. Unfortunately, most people are not good listeners, without making a conscious effort. The reason they are not good listeners is that they are not paying attention to what the other person is saying. You may recall that in a conversation you had to interrupt the speaker and say, "I'm sorry, I didn't catch your last remark." Or, "What did you say?" If so, you were not listening attentively. Lack of attention is a major conversational sin. This sin of inattention you can overcome by *concentrating on what the other person is talking about* and giving the speaker your undivided attention. You will find that effective listening is a good business tool. To listen attentively means that you are making it easier for yourself to remember all the facts and to comprehend the ideas that are being expressed. In order to work more efficiently and effectively, you must *listen to instructions* most attentively and follow them exactly. The result will be surprising. Your executive will appreciate being able to assign work to you with the secure knowledge that it will be done right.

15. A GOOD TELEPHONE PERSONALITY

With the telephone providing communication by voice, the proper tone of your voice is a primary requirement in making friends and creating good will in the business office. The friendly impression that you create on the telephone is just as important as the one you create in person. Each time you answer the telephone remember to be *friendly*. The pleasant manner in which you answer the telephone indicates that you are willing to be of service.

DETERMINE YOUR PERSONALITY WEAKNESSES

A good personality rating is a *must* for a successful secretary. Answer each of the following questions by checking "Rarely or Never," "Sometimes," or "Usually or Always" in the spaces provided under each heading.

	Rarely or Never	Some-times	Usually or Always
1. I am adaptable, intuitive, and levelheaded.	....	....	....
2. I have a good sense of humor.	....	....	....
3. I am competent and cooperative.	....	....	....
4. I am tactful, gracious, courteous, and considerate.	....	....	....
5. I speak quietly and calmly.	....	....	....
6. I respect other people's opinions.	....	....	....
7. I avoid feeling gloomy.	....	....	....
8. I resent criticism.	....	....	....
9. I am dependable in holding confidential information that should be confidential.	....	....	....
10. I am unapproachable when I am busy.	....	....	....

If you take this inventory of personality weaknesses seriously, it will provide a foundation for self-improvement. Those habits which you have checked "Rarely or Never" reveal your most serious faults. You should seize this opportunity to develop and cultivate them immediately. The check marks which you have placed in the column headed "Sometimes" also indicate weak points which should be corrected.

SUMMING UP

The valuable requirements outlined in this chapter are intended to serve as a guide to better secretarial performance that eventually leads to bigger and better opportunities. As a bright and alert secretary you know, of course, that better opportunities are the result of conscientious, hard work, and a readiness to perform as efficiently as possible in all phases of modern office routine.

To some young aspiring secretaries the road to a successful business career appears golden, indeed. Attracted by the so-called "glamour" of the business world, these young women expect to *walk into a dream job*. That is merely an illusion. The high-level secretarial positions with dynamic executives are not for "dreamers." It is the secretary who follows a steady course of purposeful action in all her endeavors who becomes the holder of the so-called "dream job."

Chapter 2

HOW TO WORK WITH
YOUR EXECUTIVE

Everything appears to be going well at your job. Suddenly Mr. Brown's voice is heard above the clatter of typewriters.

"Miss Reade!" he calls out.

Immediately, you stop what you are doing and hasten into his office. Thinking it is the usual call for dictation, you take your shorthand notebook with you.

"Where did you get this word?" Mr. Brown questions, as he points to a sentence in the carbon copy of a letter which you typed the day before. "I never said such a thing!" he exclaims.

A bit puzzled, you begin to wonder . . . "What did I do that could be wrong? I'm so glad I have my steno book with me," you think. "Now I can check my shorthand notes!"

As you read over your shorthand outlines, you see that they correspond to each word in the sentence. Feeling certain that you did not make the error, you blurt out thoughtlessly, "They *are* your words, Mr. Brown." To make the situation worse, you offer to read back your shorthand notes.

It is a mistake to try to exonerate yourself in this way. To point out your executive's error is not only embarrassing, but it *weakens his authority*.

The above situation typifies the experience of a "novice"

secretary who lacked proper training in diplomacy. Not surprisingly, she was told that her services were no longer needed.

"This experience taught me a valuable lesson," she says. "From that day on, *I learned to be more tactful.*"

Expressions such as the following should help you in a situation of this kind to insure good will between yourself and your executive:

"I'm sorry, Mr. Brown, that I made the error. I probably did not hear you correctly." Or, "I don't know how that happened, next time I shall be more careful."

A word of advice: If you're not sure of the kind of mood that your executive might be in, it is best, in the long run, to assume that he might be right. Contradicting him only creates a personality clash. If you learn to work with him, instead of competing with him, you will gain his confidence and your relations will be ever so much better.

It may be true that the secretary is her boss's greatest critic, but she *must wait until her criticisms are asked for.* Until your executive shows you that he places complete confidence in your opinions, you must make a conscious effort to avoid offending him.

To be able to understand and get along with people, you must develop your own personality in ways that will help you to build good human relations.

As a secretary, you are a member of the "executive team." It is essential that you learn how to adjust your own personality to that of your executive. In a sense, you must try to see his problems through his eyes, not your own. Also, you must try to understand his feelings. A knowledge of his work habits and preferences will enable you to complete your duties in the manner most satisfactory to him.

You may well ask, "How can I *better understand* my boss?"

STUDY YOUR EXECUTIVE

One effective approach toward achieving a more compatible relationship is to give some intensive study to the *temperament* of your executive.

Try to find answers to such questions as, "What kind of man is he?" "What are his hobbies or interests?" "Does he have a genial disposition?" "Is he quick-tempered or even-tempered?" These are all questions to which you must find answers, for it is only after you have acquired knowledge of this kind that you are able to understand and foresee how your executive is going to act.

No two persons are exactly alike. Each has his own individuality, his own peculiarities. The personality of every individual is the sum-total of his distinctive qualities expressed in his physical and mental activities and attitudes. Below is a list of the habitual patterns and qualities of behavior dominant in *ten* different types of executives. In studying your particular executive you may discover that he possesses qualities that are manifested by one or more of the following types. However, with the insight gained, you will be able to judge your executive *impartially* and to *adapt yourself* to his various moods.

1. The dynamic type, with seemingly inexhaustible energy.
It takes an equally energetic person to keep up with this executive's terrific driving force. You have to be able to work with every ounce of your vitality. You must also show initiative and, if necessary, assume considerable responsibility.

2. The slow type.
For this executive to consider you "the perfect secretary" it would be wise not to be too quick in getting out your work. Because of his own slow manner, he is probably of the opinion that it takes time to do things. A too-fast approach on your part is apt to confuse him or to make him feel self-critical.

3. The all-for-speed type.

You most likely will be more successful working with this executive if you are quick in interpreting any new idea he may conceive and putting it into operation. He has a mind which works with flash-lightning quickness and he undoubtedly expects you to keep up with him.

4. The temperamental type.

In working for this executive your main job is to keep things calm. Because he is quick-tempered, you must carefully avoid doing anything that will rouse him to anger. An atmosphere of dignity and formality on your part should keep him in good spirits.

5. The meticulous type.

You must always be on your toes when working for this executive. Everything that you do must be exact and accurate; he is apt to penalize you for the slightest evidence of poor spelling or punctuation.

6. The type who likes to concentrate on one thing at a time.

Because this executive is methodical by nature, he most likely expects you to be the same. If you are to work harmoniously with him, don't try to bring several things to his attention at once. Instead, bring each matter *separately* so that he can study and consider it in detail from every angle.

7. The conscientious, hard-working type.

You'll be able to get along with this executive if you don't mind working a little harder than most secretaries do. His persevering nature makes him somewhat of a taskmaster. Besides overworking himself, he is likely to keep you working overtime to carry out his ideas.

8. The disorganized type.

This executive needs a well-organized person around to help

keep him under control. You'll probably spend much of your time locating papers he is continually misplacing. Because he can't work differently, you'll have to accept him the way he is. Rather than trying to reform him, aim to give him all the help you can.

9. The contrary type.

You will have to train yourself to be a "yes" girl if you are working for this executive. He has a weakness for *always being right,* even about a subject he does not know too thoroughly.

10. The aggressive type.

Because he has an overpowering personality, you will probably have some difficulty putting yourself forward in any way. In order to exercise any initiative, with a man of this type, you must *first* find out if he approves.

Note: The above illustrations are intended merely to serve as a guide in building a more workable and satisfactory executive-to-secretary relationship. If you should find some flaws in your executive's image, *do not* try to reform him. Accept him as he is; keep your feelings under control.

After you have learned your executive's likes and dislikes, his strengths and weaknesses, and his ways of doing things, you will be able to anticipate all his needs. This brings us to the next important element in studying your executive—that is, *having a thorough knowledge of his functions.*

AN EXECUTIVE'S JOB

An executive is an individual who holds a position of administrative or managerial responsibility in an organization. He knows his job and what is required of him. He spends much of his time maintaining a productive and progressive office. He understands the principle of delegation of responsibility; and he surrounds himself with competent specialists who can help him in his managerial role.

The most prized possession of an executive is an efficient secretary who can help make his efforts effective. To achieve this objective, she *must know all she can about his job* and what is required of him personally. Depending upon the kind of position your executive holds in the company, the following are *ten* important executive responsibilities with which he may be directly involved:

1. He gets things running smoothly by careful planning.

2. He delegates responsibilities and makes sure someone is regularly assigned to each task.

3. He seeks counsel and advice from his associates and superiors.

4. He encourages enthusiasm, initiative, and creative thinking by showing a willingness to accept new ideas from his subordinates.

5. He maintains a "control system" which enables him to check up on chores that need follow-through.

6. He sets up guidelines for handling human relations problems.

7. He engages in *positive thinking* and does not make a decision until a situation absolutely demands it.

8. He attends company board meetings.

9. He maintains a satisfactory client or customer relationship.

10. He attends local or out-of-town conventions, as well as meetings of business associations and councils, as either a member or a guest speaker.

These are only part of the mounting executive functions. As a competent secretary, you know, of course, that merely having a thorough knowledge of your executive's duties serves no purpose unless you develop yourself to meet the requirements of your job.

YOUR ROLE AS SECRETARY

The search for good secretaries goes on all the time. Executives are always looking for highly skilled, poised secretaries who can accept responsibility, and who are able to play an important role in the managerial process as well. Because management techniques have taken on new proportions, the executive's job, today, is becoming more and more complex. He must work harder. He must have more and more know-how and leadership. But all of this leadership, ambition, and talent is worthless unless he knows in which direction he is going.

Acting as his "double" and thinking as nearly as possible along the same lines as he does, you can help steer your executive on the right course and make his work a lot easier for him. The following are areas in which you can increase your effectiveness on the job.

ANTICIPATE YOUR EXECUTIVE'S NEEDS

As a secretary who possesses foresight and good judgment, you will be able to serve your executive well. To be of greatest value to him and to anticipate his every need, you must *first* find out how he likes things done. This may be accomplished by *observing, listening,* and *asking questions.* By showing an eagerness to learn all you can about your executive's functions, you are exhibiting a genuine desire to reach out and enlarge your capacity. This means that you have a curiosity about what goes on in your job. It also indicates that you have initiative to exercise your skills and abilities on your own. You are cooperating with your executive intelligently and professionally, when you help free his mind of worry by looking ahead and performing certain duties before he makes the request. For example:

Help prepare him for meetings. You will please your executive if you come to work fifteen or twenty minutes earlier than usual, especially on a day when he has an early morning meeting scheduled. During the extra time, you can check up on some last-minute details, such as the following:

1. Whether the meeting is to be held in a formal conference room or in your executive's office, where a conference table has been set up for the purpose, have available for each person attending such items as pads, well-sharpened pencils, and ash trays.

2. So that the meeting will start as scheduled, call by telephone everyone who is expected to attend and remind him of the time and place.

3. If special reports, letters, or other material will be used at the meeting, have them ready for your executive to take with him.

4. Obtain any special equipment that will be needed, such as: a slide projector, a tape recorder, and the like.

Helping your executive, even in small ways, enables him to function better and more effectively.

Place incoming mail on his desk just as soon as possible. Some secretaries regard the matter of opening and sorting the mail as a minor task which requires little or no effort. Efficient handling of the mail *is essential* if you are to help your executive perform effectively in the important area of business letter-writing. When the mail comes in, here is what you do:

1. Open it immediately (and stamp "date received," if this is a standard practice in your office) and place it in a neat pile on your executive's desk or in the box marked "Incoming Mail."

2. You can help cut down his reading time if you put top priority items on top.

3. If some letters are replies to previous correspondence, you can help him quickly to bring himself up to date on the subject if you clip the newly-received replies to the file copies of the correspondence and bring them to his attention.

As a secretary who handles all tasks efficiently, you can save your executive a great deal of time so that he can devote more of his day to executive planning, thinking, and acting.

Help him to work more effectively. A competent secretary

never misses the opportunity to help her executive to be more effective on the job. As a well-read person, you will be able to bring to your executive's attention any newspaper item or magazine article that may be useful to him in connection with his work. For example, if he is preparing a report, you can save him considerable amount of research if you give him the trade magazine article you came upon which contains helpful information he could use in his report.

Reading opens the doors to many avenues of thinking, and here is an instance in which good reading habits can pay you dividends. You can be certain of one thing: Your executive will greatly appreciate the interest that you show to help him perform better.

Keep him informed as to what is going on. In every office interesting and exciting events are always taking place. Because your executive is so busy with his work, he sometimes misses the opportunity of becoming aware of such information as: (a) the names of new employees; (b) exciting events that have happened to employees or other executives; (c) office visits by former employees or executives, particularly such persons as he would like very much to see.

It may be that the company's former Executive Vice President is back for a visit and is in the vicinity of your executive's office. It will benefit your executive to know that this special visitor is about, particularly if he is expected to stop by to say "hello." When the former Executive Vice President finally arrives, your executive will have had sufficient time to think up some appropriate topics to discuss with him. Preparing your executive ahead of time for such a visit can save him the embarrassment of a "cold greeting" and of having to struggle for something to say.

You may think that keeping your executive informed as to what is going on may be classed as "office gossip," but actually it is not, for you are helping to build better working and human relationships for your executive. Conversation is the basis for the miracle of communication. And talking with people is not only fun; it is good for us as social human beings. Of course, you don't have to discuss everything you see or hear with your executive. As a secretary who possesses good judgment, you will be able to recognize the difference between mere gossip and the kind of information that your executive really should have.

Set up a tickler system for remembering things. A "tickler" is a device for jogging the memory. Specifically, it is a dated file which serves as a reminder and is arranged to bring matters to timely attention. With such a device functioning, you can easily jog your executive's memory, as well as your own.

For quick reference, keep the tickler file in your desk drawer or in a nearby file cabinet. It should contain thirty-one file folders, numbered from 1 to 31, that is, one file folder for each day of the month. Put in each of these file folders, as a reminder, those items that you and/or your executive want to remember on that particular day.

For instance, let's assume that your executive is scheduled to present a Marketing Report at the Plans Board Meeting on September 15. So that he will have the report ready for that day, this is what you do:

1. Type on a sheet of paper this reminder: *Marketing Report due at Plans Board Meeting September 15.*
2. Next, put the sheet of paper in the file folder marked No. 10 (for September 10), five days before that particular meeting.
3. Then, on September 10, remove the No. 10 File Folder from your tickler file and put it on your executive's desk so that he can be aware of which items are pending. When he sees your note regarding the Plans Board Meeting, he will be reminded that he has these five days in which to prepare the report.

Note: So that your tickler system will function with complete accuracy, at the end of each day, put the tickler file folder for that particular day behind the last folder in the file.

For example, suppose that today is September 1, and you have taken care of all the pending items that you had placed in the No. 1 File Folder.

1. Put the No. 1 File Folder behind the No. 31 File Folder. Thus, File Folder No. 2 will come up next for handling on September 2.

2. Then, on September 2, after you have taken care of any pending items in File Folder No. 2, put the File Folder No. 2 behind File Folder No. 1. Thus, File Folder No. 3 will come up next for handling on September 3.

3. Repeat this procedure with all thirty-one file folders, until File Folder No. 1 again appears at the beginning of the number sequence, ready to start the month of October.

Note: For those months that have thirty days, it will be necessary to skip the No. 31 File Folder which you already have set up and begin the next month with the No. 1 File Folder.

Keep him posted as to what is going on when he is away. If your executive is away from the office for several days on a business trip, he will most likely be interested in what is happening during his absence. Sending him a running *diary of events* is an excellent means by which you can keep him up to the minute on the day-to-day events that are taking place at the office. In preparing a diary schedule, it is not necessary, however, to inform your executive of every little item that comes up. If you did, he would be overburdened with a lot of unnecessary reading. Instead, keep it simple, as well as informative, and include only those items that are of importance or interest to him. For example:

Diary of Events
Monday, October 3
1. Mr. Smith of ABC Tool Company telephoned. Would like very much to talk with you. Will call you again when you return.
2. A Plans Review Board meeting is set for October 18 at 9:30 A.M. in the Directors' Room. Those ex-

pected to attend: J. Jones, P. Peterson, M. Came-
ron, *W. Brown* (underline your executive's name).
3. John Avery is preparing the Marketing Plan for
ABC Tool Co. As soon as it is typed, he will send
it to you, air mail, in L.A., along with a memo ex-
plaining some details.

Tuesday, October 4
(List of items)

Wednesday, October 5
(List of items)

Such a schedule of events can be of great value to your
executive in aiding him to increase his personal effectiveness on
the job, even while he is away.

1. It helps to keep him informed on active matters.
2. He has an opportunity to give his final approval on important data that need immediate action.
3. Because he already has knowledge of matters that have
come up while he was away, when he returns he is able to focus
his full attention on the work to be done immediately.

It is the aim of every competent secretary to help her executive make the best possible use of his time and effort, and you
can do this by looking ahead and anticipating your executive's
every need.

COPE WITH YOUR EXECUTIVE'S WORK HABITS

The first step to be taken by any secretary is to become acquainted with her executive's method of doing things. As already
indicated, no two bosses work in exactly the same manner. Each
has his own individual and peculiar methods.

One secretary reports: "My boss prefers to open the mail
himself. Because he is methodical by nature, he likes to open each
letter separately and give the subject matter his immediate attention. I've been working with him for some time, now, and the

only time he wants me to open the mail is when he is away on a business trip or on vacation. When he returns to the office, I go back to placing the mail on his desk unopened. I accept this peculiarity of his because he has other essential qualities that to my mind rate him 'tops' as an executive."

Another relates: "My executive prefers to keep his own calendar up to date regarding meetings and luncheon appointments. During dictation, he asks me to make a note of such items so that I may keep up to date on his activities. Sometimes he forgets to tell me about a luncheon appointment. To be sure that I have knowledge of all his activities, I check through his calendar when he isn't around, and make a note for myself of any item that I do not already have."

Whatever peculiarity your executive may possess, be as wise as these two secretaries and adapt yourself to his wishes. No one is perfect, and no one expects you to be either. Peculiarities are bound to show up in every individual, and your executive is no exception. If you criticize him, even in your own mind, you will only make the situation worse.

Since the secretary's main function is to keep her executive happy, you should find out how your executive wants everything done. Rather than trying to force your ways on him, you should learn to adjust your work habits and your personality to his and adapt yourself to his peculiar work preferences.

Help him to be more effective on the telephone

Much of today's business starts and ends with the telephone. Since the telephone is one of the important business instruments used by everyone, it is essential that it be used skillfully and effectively to win the good will of the caller. Very often, the caller will base his image of a company on his reaction to the first person who answers him. Companies spend enormous sums of money to build a good "corporate image." And then one poor telephone contact can (a) result in the loss of millions of dollars, or (b) destroy a good image which had been built up over the years.

Your executive plays an important role in maintaining the

reputation of your company, as well as his own, in the best possible light in the minds of clients or customers. In your supporting role as secretary, you are expected to cooperate with him whenever a situation provides the opportunity. It is only through experience and good judgment that you will be able to carry on your work and, at the same time, to listen to your executive's telephone conversations, to be on hand to help him. For example, suppose that your executive is talking on the telephone with an important client. You know that a certain document which you filed the other day contains just the information that he needs. He will be able to conduct his telephone conversation more efficiently, if you can extract the document from the files as quickly as possible, and place it so that he can have the information at his fingertips. The skill which you exhibit in assisting your executive to be more effective on the telephone is another step toward proving your worth as an efficient secretary.

EXERCISE INITIATIVE WITHOUT BEING AGGRESSIVE

Top-level secretaries show initiative by using their heads. But they must know how to function without creating resentment.

In your role as secretary, you are continually on the lookout for new and better ways of aiding your executive. In some instances, it is necessary for you to inject your thoughts which may be beneficial to his work. The more you are able to do this, the more valuable you make yourself. But, at the same time, you must be careful not to convey the slightest impression that you are trying to step into his shoes.

Most executives encourage creative thinking. However, if you do undertake originating any new idea or suggestion, you will want to make certain that your executive will take a favorable view of it. You can do this by asking yourself in advance these four questions:

	Answers
1. Is my idea invited?	(YES)
2. Does it make sense?	(YES)
3. Am I correct in my thinking?	(YES)
4. Will it offend him in any way?	(NO)

If you are able to provide the correct answers to the above questions, you stand a good chance to express your thoughts intelligently, creatively, and artistically. On the other hand, if you fail to answer each question correctly, then what you intend to suggest is probably not as effective as you think it is. Under these circumstances, to avoid a possible conflict of personalities, it is best not to say anything at all.

This self-examination should serve as a yardstick for judging in advance how receptive your executive will be to any suggestion you may wish to make. The next step is to introduce your idea without appearing to be aggressive. A good way to do this is to put it in the form of a question. You can say in effect: "May I take a minute to discuss an idea regarding the Marketing Plan that I believe will be helpful to you?"

If your executive is interested: (a) he will ask you to tell him immediately; or (b) he will ask you to wait until he has a free moment; or (c) he will ask you to put your thoughts in a memo.

Once he realizes that your sole aim is to help him to be more productive on the job, your executive most likely will seek your assistance on such matters as could benefit by your particular thoughts or talents.

A word of advice: After you gain your executive's confidence in your opinions, don't make the mistake of thinking he is obliged to accept all your suggestions. Remember, you are not always right in your thinking. If your executive should reject one of your suggestions, his main reason probably is his belief that the suggestion is impractical and could not be carried out successfully.

BUILD UP HIS "EXECUTIVE IMAGE"

A good secretary knows instinctively what to do to bring out the best in her executive through her own actions. She knows, too, that it is up to her to adapt herself to his ways and conduct herself with dignity at all times.

In your role as secretary you have the obligation of making the best possible use of your abilities and devoting all your energies toward building a more workable executive-secretary relationship.

As you learn to know your executive, you will know more and more how he normally thinks and acts. You will know his moods and his reactions. While he expects you to think along the same lines as he does, he expects you to be one step ahead of him all the time. Certainly, your biggest problem here will be to exercise discretion so as not to appear forward or pushing, in any way. However, after you have studied your executive's likes and dislikes, his moods and his ways of doing things, then working with him in harmony becomes easier and more natural.

Be his memory. Because your executive is under constant pressure, it is almost impossible for him to remember every little detail. He will come to depend upon the role that *your* memory plays in helping him perform in the most efficient manner.

Before you start jogging your executive's memory, determine first how and when he likes to be reminded.

a. If you are reminding your executive for the first time, and you feel that reminding him might conceivably be an insult to the perfect memory that he thinks he has, be subtle in your approach and bring things to his attention gently and quietly.

b. If he prefers to receive notes, then present your reminder in a note.

c. If it is in the morning that he wants to be reminded of things when his mind is free of details, tell him then.

Following are areas in which you can help your executive to use his memory more effectively:

1. If your executive comments that he wants to send Mr. Willard some figures next Monday regarding the J. C. Allen Construction Corporation contract, record it immediately on your calendar. (This may be his way of telling you that he wants you to help him to remember.) Then, when you remind him on Monday, as an extra service to him, you can have the information

already outlined in a memo. Your executive will be most grateful to know that you not only assisted him to remember, but that you also saved him the time to compile the information himself.

2. Keep his calendar current. Make notes of meetings and appointments. Then by a gentle reminder, you can see that he doesn't forget his appointments. Also, that he gets to meetings on time.

3. Have the necessary material for meetings ready, such as letters, reports, exhibits, statistical data, and the like.

4. Prepare an itinerary—a travel diary of his out-of-town trips. Items to be recorded are: (a) departure and arrival time of both the going and the return trip; (b) manner of travel— plane, train, or hired car (if he prefers to drive); (c) hotel address and telephone number, type of reservation, and room number.

These are just a few instances in which you can activate your executive's memory. Of course, because your position is determined by the particular job that your executive holds in the company, you may encounter many other situations in which your memory can play a major role in keeping your executive's mind free of worry and/or details so he can devote more of his time to planning and thinking.

Respect his weaknesses or errors. Whenever possible, cover up for him. For example, due to pressure of work, your executive may erroneously set up two luncheon appointments for the same day. Here is where your secretarial skill can go into action. You must be able to cancel one of these two appointments with the *utmost tact.* The situation may be handled in the following manner:

Call the secretary of the man whose appointment is to be cancelled and say . . . "This is Miss Reade, Mr. Brown's secretary. Mr. Brown is very sorry that he will not be able to keep his luncheon appointment with Mr. Deal today. An emergency meeting has arisen which won't break up before noon. Under the circumstances, he hopes that Mr. Deal will understand."

Once your executive realizes your ability to save him from embarrassment, he will regard you as a valuable asset. And he will come to rely on your secretarial ingenuity to free him from other involving situations.

Know where to locate him. Your executive may at times be careless about informing you of his whereabouts. Also you may be so engrossed in what you are doing that you don't realize he is not in his office. Nonetheless, if such is the case, when a top man or an important client inquires where your executive is, *never* say that you don't know. *It is up to you to keep track of him.* And also to make certain that he is readily accessible to the right people.

A conscientious effort on your part to observe your executive's activities will enable you to develop an "uncanny intuition" as to his whereabouts. Following are two suggestions for improving your secretarial sleuthing:

1. *Time his activities.* Perhaps your executive usually does his banking in the morning, say about 11 A.M. Observe how long it usually takes him to perform the errand. Then, if an emergency situation should develop, and he has neglected to tell you where he will be, you will know instinctively that he is at the bank and that he won't be away too long.

2. *Know his contacts.* If it is necessary for your executive to visit several people in order to follow through on his assignments, keep a list of their names and telephone numbers or extensions handy so that you can reach him immediately. Put the names of those persons whom he frequently visits at the top of the list. Here's the experience of one secretary whose executive was in the habit of not leaving word where he was going: When an important client telephoned, all she had to do was call each person on her list, until she was successful in tracking him down. Amazed that she was able to locate him each time, her executive asked one day how she knew where to find him. Reluctant about giving away her "trade secret," she quickly replied, "I rely upon my woman's intuition."

Help him keep up with routine work. Routine work *is* important, and since some parts are detailed, time is required in handling it. Because your executive might be involved with other important work, he will sometimes set aside a routine chore until he has finished something on which he must concentrate more thoroughly. To prevent him from falling behind in his work, you can be most helpful if you will take over the handling of certain routine chores. Telephone calls concerning routine matters can also be handled by you. Your desire and ability to assist your executive in every way possible will help him to maintain a high standard of performance in everything he does.

Protect him from unimportant matters

Some secretaries find that their most important duty is protecting their executive's time, keeping his mind free of worry about details by disposing of the details themselves.

As a well-trained secretary, you are expected to protect your executive from unimportant matters. There are times when you will be required to handle the trivial tasks that your executive is bogged down with whenever he is under pressure with important work. Utilizing your administrative ability, you can do such things as the following:

1. Answer requests for information and supply the data; but be sure that you let your executive know what you are doing.
2. Handle follow-throughs on routine work. If the matter can be dealt with verbally, telephone the proper person. If a written follow-up is necessary, outline your thoughts in a memo.
3. Screen all telephone calls and be sure that your executive returns the urgent calls the first chance he gets.

Your readiness to be of assistance is a key factor in your efforts to support your executive and see that his job responsibilities are carried out efficiently. This becomes another reason for him to rate you as an "efficient secretary."

KEEP CONFIDENTIAL CONVERSATIONS TO YOURSELF

Keeping confidential matters to herself is of prime importance among the functions of a secretary.

It is a bad habit to start rumors anywhere. It is a great mistake, in an office, to think that you should discuss everything you hear with your fellow-workers. Your executive's confidential remarks to you *are not to be treated as news items.* If he intended his conversations with you to be the concern of everyone, he would have them issued in a general office memorandum. So whatever you see or hear, *keep it to yourself.*

Here is a plan you can follow in resisting the temptation of disclosing any "top-secret" information.

Suppose that you accidentally overheard one of your executive's confidential discussions. The thing to do is to *pretend that you did not hear anything. And do not repeat it.* Just forget about it until the matter reaches the others in the office. This little game of challenge never fails. You are the winner every time! Besides proving to yourself that you *can keep a secret,* you can be certain that you *did not start a rumor.*

Another advantage of this plan is that your executive will know that he can rely on you to keep all confidential matters "top secret," as they should be.

REFER TO THE FILES, THE OFFICE "TREASURE CHEST"

A smart secretary who desires to learn *more* about her job is well aware that the files hold a *wealth of information* that will be of great value to her in solving most of the routine problems. It requires patience and determination to read through the filed correspondence; but in your efforts to delve through this valuable source of information, you will find many helpful hints that will add to your efficiency.

1. You will learn more about your company's policy and procedure.

2. You will become thoroughly familiar with the nature of the business.

3. You will learn special phraseology and terminology regarding the company product.

4. You will learn from past correspondence how your executive expresses his thoughts and ideas in writing.

5. You will find helpful information that may be of value to you at some future time.

Each chance you get to refer to the files is another opportunity to learn more about the business. Through what you learn you will be better prepared to meet your challenging job.

Turn out a quantity of work under pressure, if necessary

A good secretary is expected by her executive to turn out a quantity of work accurately whenever the situation demands it.

Some secretaries often complain: "When I'm rushed and have a lot of work to do, I find that I make mistakes." If you are like these secretaries, fretting won't get you anywhere. Why not do something about it?

As a qualified secretary, you have a great deal to offer. The skills you have mastered are the tools of your trade. But your attitudes, your attributes of mind and character, and your personal disciplines are just as essential if you are to function effectively and professionally.

If you find that your duties have plagued you beyond what seems to be the level of your capacity, remember this: (1) be calm; (2) think clearly; (3) perform each task in the order of its importance.

Once you have learned to approach your work with complete confidence, you won't feel the volume and pressure of your job. You'll be able to turn out top-quality work, even when you are rushed. And the occasional "extra duties" that you are asked to perform will not seem too burdensome. Your executive will be pleased to have a secretary who is able to help him take care of the important, rush assignments that occasionally turn up.

DEVELOP A PLEASING PERSONALITY

A pleasing personality is an essential business asset.

Many executives view the secretary as an "expert" in her field. In addition to keeping the quality of her performance at a high level, she must, in order to be regarded as "the perfect secretary," be *charmingly beautiful, delightfully pleasant,* and *gracefully energetic.* Let us define these requirements:

Charmingly beautiful may sound a bit confusing. If you think that you must have outstanding physical beauty to be a secretary, you are wrong. The truth is, with the aid of cosmetics, we are today able to make ourselves "look" attractive. Natural beauty is a God-given gift. However, those few people who are exceptionally good looking, have a tendency to lack charm and personality. Because they *know* they are beautiful, they sometimes become vain and self-centered. This kind of beauty may be called "external beauty." It is only skin deep. On the other hand, those people who do not possess extraordinary beauty are the ones who can be exuberant with charm and personality. The reason is that Mother Nature failed them in one way and is making up for the imperfection in another way. Therefore, the *charm* which they exhibit so abundantly, is what *makes them beautiful.* This kind of beauty may be called "internal beauty." Just as a volcano belches out from its depths, the rich minerals that are hidden beneath the earth's surface, Mother Nature generously pours forth *from her heart* all her warmth and sincere goodness. In other words, beauty without charm has very little real value.

Delightfully pleasant is exactly what you should make every effort to be. A friendly attitude goes a long way in building better human relations. In fact, it is a *must* if you are employed in a large organization where among a great many people differences of personality are a factor. Your ability to work harmoniously with the other members in your office is of paramount importance. Three essential reminders which will help you to call forth and exert good will are: (1) Always be pleasant and willing to be of assistance, whenever possible. (2) Treat the other fellow as you would like to be treated if you were in his place. (3) *Never* be discourteous or ill-tempered. For example: If someone should ask you a question pertaining to the work, it is rude merely to say, "I can't speak to you right now" or "I'm busy, come back a little later." Remarks such as these give the following impressions: (a) that you are emotionally immature, (b) that you are placing greater importance upon your job than the other fellow's, and (c) that you are disagreeable and hard to get along with. Instead of making friends, you are creating enemies. People will think that you are deliberately unfriendly. Your good office behavior, therefore, is a prime essential. If you will remember to be pleasant and friendly *at all times* you will gain the respect and admiration of everyone, *especially your executive.* Below is a note of thanks one secretary received from her executive in appreciation of her excellent cooperation and loyalty to him.

> In the trying pressure-job we live in, it becomes a habit to be out of sorts and harassed. Yet it can truly be said that you have never been anything but delightfully pleasant, efficient, and faithful. This factor alone, is ever so important. The days were made so much easier and more enjoyable.

To be told that you are *delightfully pleasant* is, indeed, one of the nicest compliments anyone can pay you.

Gracefully energetic may sound like an unusual attribute. Actually, to be gracefully energetic is not as difficult as it sounds. In order to retain a well-composed appearance throughout the day, you must be able to exert the energy that is required to complete your assignments without working yourself to a point of exhaustion. You might ask, "How is this possible?" The answer, of course, is simply this: (1) Be calm, (2) Think calmly, and (3) Look calm. If you *are calm,* you will be able to perform your work without strain or tension. If you *think calmly,* you will be able to approach your work more intelligently. And if you *look calm,* you will show that you are efficient. Besides helping you to control your emotions, the following exercise, if put to memory, will enable you to create the right impression.

C—is for cheerfulness
A—is for amiable
L—is for likable
M—is for magnetic

It is quite obvious that the word "calm" is the *key* to your emotional stability. The easygoing manner in which you handle your assignments indicates that you have poise and self-assurance.

SUMMARY

Your willingness to be of assistance in many ways is the *secret* to a better understanding of your executive.

The efforts that you undertake in creating good will between yourself and your executive will work to your advantage. An agreeable personality will let you radiate an attitude which *attracts* and *pleases.*

Once you have learned ways to better understand your executive, you will be able to fit in with his work habits and work with him as a team. The results are surprising. You will be able to anticipate his thoughts. In many instances, he will come to seek your opinion and advice.

Because you have gained your executive's confidence, he will place *utmost trust* in you. And he can proudly say, *"I have a most efficient secretary!"* This is the finest compliment your executive can pay you.

Chapter 3

18 WAYS TO AVOID

OFFICE FATIGUE

A GOOD RULE TO REMEMBER

As your duties increase, you must find ways to conserve your time and energy so as to be able to perform your work untiringly.

To exemplify the importance of this rule, I'd like to relate the following conversation:

Two secretaries were wondering how a third secretary in their office, Miss Reade, accomplished her work.

"Miss Reade," one of them said, "you're always busy. Yet you look so fresh and calm. What's your secret?"

"There isn't any secret," Miss Reade told the two secretaries. And she related the following story of how she was able to perform her work efficiently without showing any signs of fatigue.

Miss Reade said that she used to work for a New York Sales Representative. The office staff consisted of two assistants and three secretaries. Miss Reade was secretary to one of the assistants.

Although her duties were not too hectic, she found at the

beginning that she became tired by the end of every day. And when she had an important job to do, she would easily become nervous and upset. Then everything she did would be wrong. And the harder she tried not to make an error, the more mistakes she would make. Of the three secretaries in the office, Miss Reade seemed to be the only one who was having this difficulty.

She began to observe Miss Johnson, her employer's secretary. Miss Johnson was always poised and calm, busily performing her duties. She was a woman in her late 30's, about 38. She could attend to everything that came up in the office from taking dictation to operating the switchboard. She also performed her own work very skillfully. And the important jobs she handled most efficiently.

Miss Reade wondered why she wasn't able to perform her duties the way Miss Johnson performed hers. She was determined to find out.

So one day Miss Reade said to Miss Johnson, "Miss Johnson, I admire the way you get your work done, You always accomplish all your assignments so expertly. I wish I could handle my job as well as you do. Won't you please tell me what I am doing that seems to be wrong?"

To this Miss Johnson replied: "Miss Reade, I do believe I can be of some help. I've noticed that you get upset very easily, especially when you have a rush job to do. This is wrong. All you gain at the end of the day are tense nerves that use up most of your energy. Instead, you must try to be calm. The calmer you are, the more work you'll be able to perform. And *the more responsibilities you are able to handle, the more you'll be recognized as competent.*"

"What must I do if I have more work than I can handle?" asked Miss Reade.

"That's simple," answered Miss Johnson, *"as your duties increase, you must find ways to conserve your time and energy so that you'll be able to perform your work without getting tired."*

At first Miss Reade found this advice a bit unusual. She had expected that Miss Johnson would give her some ideas and techniques on just *how* she should handle her work. Instead, Miss

Johnson stressed the importance of her finding ways to conserve her time and energy in order to be able to perform her work UNTIRINGLY.

The first thing Miss Reade did was to examine her abilities to pinpoint the source of her difficulty. So she wrote the following heading on a sheet of paper and set down ten questions under it.

HOW DO YOU RATE YOUR PERFORMANCE?

You can determine just where your most serious weaknesses lie. Check "yes" or "no" in the spaces provided after each question. Five NO's, your performance is fair. Six or more NO's, then you should resolve to apply high standards to your work and to correct weaknesses which fall short of these standards.

	YES	NO
1. Do you listen carefully to instructions?	....	....
2. Do you carry out instructions exactly as they have been given?	....	....
3. Do you ask questions when things are not clear to you?	....	....
4. Is your desk neat and well organized as you work?	....	....
5. Do you perform each task in order of priority?	....	....
6. Do you transcribe the most important letters first?	....	....
7. Do you use a follow-up system to follow through on projects?	....	....
8. Can you find wanted papers and important documents in your files quickly?	....	....

9. Do you have the ability to assume responsibility when the situation demands it? ....

10. Do you have the ability to perform your special skills in any segment of your company? ....

If you take this inventory of work habits seriously, it not only will indicate your most serious faults, but it also will provide a foundation for self-improvement.

The result of this examination of herself was instructive for Miss Reade. After giving each question considerable thought, much to her chagrin, the "no" answers outnumbered the "yes" answers. With such a poor rating, she wondered if she would ever be a successful secretary. Miss Reade then began to realize that perhaps Miss Johnson was right. She immediately decided to find better ways to handle her work to improve her performance.

Miss Reade's experience emphasizes the importance of applying high standards to your work if you are to function expertly and effectively at your job.

STUDY YOUR JOB

In order to accomplish your work with greater skill, it is essential that you *study your job*. A better understanding of your work will help you along the road to success. The more efficiently you are able to handle your assignments, the more successful you are likely to be.

Ask any business executive what he expects from a good secretary and his answer will probably be: "the utmost." There's not the slightest doubt that he expects much more of her than first-class shorthand and typewriting ability.

She must have a good memory . . . an orderly mind . . . tact . . . discretion . . . and absolute loyalty to her employer.

Said one sales executive: "The manner in which my secretary performs her work enables me to determine how well she knows her job."

There are two kinds of secretaries: (1) the type who desires to better herself by being as efficient as possible; and (2) the type who prefers to stand still in the kind and amount of service she is rendering. The difference between the two is that the first makes her position greater than she found it; and the second keeps it where she found it, or doesn't keep it.

Nearly every secretary knows the fundamentals and principles of secretarial work, but to this knowledge she has got to add those little refinements which will make her work better.

EIGHT WAYS TO KEEP YOUR WORK AT A HIGH LEVEL

1. Plan your work for the day.

Careful planning of your work is essential. Before you begin, it is a good idea to make a mental picture of the order in which you will handle your assignments. If necessary, write out a simple outline to guide you. This way, you will be able to know exactly what duties you are to perform and exactly how you will perform them.

2. Know what is important and what is not important.

The ability to differentiate the big and important jobs from the little and less important ones is a great advantage. Once you have done this, you will be able to complete your daily routine more expertly.

a. The tasks which have priority should be taken care of first.

b. Work which requires more time and concentration should be taken care of when you are not too busy.

c. The morning is usually the best time to clear up details. At that time you are well rested after a good night's sleep; and your mind is fresh and free from tension. Besides, there is less

chance of distraction which will prevent you from finishing your
tasks.

3. Develop a good memory.

A good memory is a *must* if you are to accomplish your
work efficiently and accurately. Few people are gifted with the
capacity for remembering. Those who are less fortunate must
learn ways to develop a good memory.

In order to approach your work more intelligently, it would
be wise to get into the habit of writing everything down. For
example: Keep your shorthand notebook (or a memo pad) in a
convenient spot on your desk. Mark on it a heading such as
"Things to do." As soon as you are asked to perform any particular assignment, *write it down*. At that moment, you might be
and probably are, busy with something else. By making a note of
all the items you are asked to perform, you eliminate any chance
of forgetting. And as you complete each assignment, check it off
in red pencil on your "Things to do" list. This method of double-
checking has an advantage: *You are certain nothing is forgotten.*

Writing notes to yourself is also helpful. For instance: On
any correspondence which is "pending" write in the upper left-
hand corner of the letter or memo a reminder such as "Hear from
Mr. Smith," "Get schedule from Mr. Jones," or "Await approval
from Mr. Blank," etc. Reminders such as these will enable you
to see at a glance the next step of performance before you
finalize any letter or document for filing. By constantly training
yourself to remember, *you will learn to develop an orderly mind.*

4. Use proper "work tools" (office equipment).

Skillful use of proper "work tools" will add to your efficiency.

Famous painters, like Michelangelo, Rembrandt, and Leo-
nardo da Vinci, had to know how to apply the right blend of
colors to be able to create their great masterpieces.

Like these masters, the secretary, too, must have the ability
to put her secretarial skills to good use to be able to create an
atmosphere of efficiency. Know how to utilize your "work tools"

to the best advantage. This will enable you to perform your work better.

Although both the secretary's shorthand notebook and pencil have become the symbol of her profession, there are other items of office equipment which she must depend on in order to do her job right. They are:

Eraser—You may not believe it, but the eraser has a definite role to play in your secretarial career. Because it is important, it is essential that you include it among your supplies. Select a good eraser which will make a neat correction on your typewritten work. Errors that are still visible annoy the reader. He will get the following impressions: (1) that you are not a competent secretary, and (2) that your executive is not concerned with the appearance of the work you turn out for him.

Stationery, envelopes, and carbon paper—To be able to work with greater speed and efficiency, it will be helpful if you keep your supply of stationery, envelopes, and carbon paper within easy reach in your desk. Whether you use carbon paper or carbon sets, never allow your supply to become depleted. If you have to stop in the midst of an assignment to replenish it, you will lose valuable time.

A brief word regarding carbon paper. To be able to obtain clear copies of your typewritten work, avoid using carbon paper that is old and worn. Once it has been used a number of times, it will produce only blurred and unreadable copies.

Miscellaneous items—Miscellaneous items also play a role in helping you to perform your work more skillfully. The items most frequently used are: telephone message pads, labels, clips, staples, typewriter ribbons, and scotch tape. In addition to these, there are many other labor-saving devices which may be obtained at any good stationery supply store.

5. Assemble the next day's assignments the day before.
Assembling the next day's assignments the day before is

another habit worth your while. At the end of each day, pile up on your desk, or in a "pending" file folder, the things that are to be taken care of the next day. Remember to place the important assignments on top. Stacking your work *in order of priority* has these two advantages: a. You are certain that the important tasks get completed first. b. You don't have to take time to read over your work to find out which assignment needs immediate attention.

The above system can be used efficiently by most secretaries. However, some secretaries, because of the confidential nature of their work, find it necessary at the close of the day to store uncompleted assignments in a safe place. The secret spot could be in a locked file cabinet, in a safe (if you are handling money or checks), or in a special compartment inside your desk.

If you must conceal your work in order to safeguard its secrecy, be sure that you let your executive (or some other person of authority) know where you keep it. This is important for the following reasons:

a. If you should be away from the office he will be able to take care of anything that might be important.

b. If you fail to inform him where you keep your work he will have to search the office in order to locate it.

c. If he is not successful in locating your work he will have to telephone you at home in order to find out where you stored it.

d. He will lose valuable time in his search to locate your work.

6. *Handle one task at a time.*

Handling one task at a time is another method that pays off. This way you are sure to get things done quickly and accurately. Don't be the type of secretary who jumps from one task to another. If you do that, you will gain nothing but tense nerves at the end of the day. It is sensible and efficient to remain poised and calm. No executive will want you to be his secretary if you do your work in a confused manner. He will consider you incapable of handling responsibilities.

Also, keeping your desk cluttered with a lot of work that does not need immediate attention creates disorder. And disorderliness leads to confusion. For example: You may either misplace important correspondence or inadvertently mail it out along with other correspondence. To avoid making errors that are both time-consuming and embarrassing, it is best that you set aside the things that do not need immediate attention. By placing the non-rush chores out of the' way, temporarily, until you are ready to take care of them, you will be able to concentrate on one task at a time.

7. Listen carefully to instructions.

One of the most important of your secretarial functions is *listening*. The more effectively you are able to carry out instructions, the more successful you will be. We have already mentioned that some people are not good listeners. The poor listener may possess perfect hearing, yet when he is spoken to, he becomes a lifeless form. His face is expressionless, and his mind is blank. As a result, the speaker feels as if he were talking to himself. The trouble is, the poor listener pays *no attention* to what the speaker is saying. The secret to good listening is *careful listening*. By listening carefully to instructions, you have a much better chance of understanding everything. And if you understand everything, you are much more apt to remember all the pertinent facts.

How does one become a good listener?

It is simple. Here are two rules that will stimulate you to more effective listening.

When you are spoken to—

a. Your face should show that you are interested, alert and alive, by a gleam in your eye or a slight smile.

b. Keep your ears open and listen attentively.

If you will make it a practice to apply these simple rules in all your activities, you will learn to be *more attentive*. By giving your undivided attention, at all times, you will also improve your power of concentration.

This brings us to the final point in keeping your work at a high level—that is, *your ability to follow instructions.*

8. Carry out instructions exactly as they have been given.

When you are given instructions, you should make every effort to concentrate on what your executive is saying. This way, you are sure not to miss his exact meaning. If you fail to follow his instructions and complete your assignment incorrectly, you will have to perform it all over again. Each time you re-do your work, you become more exhausted. To consume all your energy needlessly on a single, simple assignment is a waste of time. It is wise to conserve your energy for the tasks which require you to exert more effort.

If you are to perform your work accurately with the least amount of effort, it would be good to have your shorthand notebook (or a small scratch pad) handy so that you can write down all the assignments that you are asked to perform. Once you have done this you will be in a position to complete each task correctly according to your executive's instructions. However, if there is anything that you do not understand, don't hesitate to ask questions. Asking questions offers these advantages:

    a. You will get a better understanding of your duties.

    b. You will save valuable time by not having to do work over, to retype letters, schedules, and so on.

    c. You will be able to produce a better quality of work.

    d. You will let your executive know that you want to do the job right.

A final and important suggestion: Whatever assignment you are asked to perform, *do it right the first time.*

TEN WAYS TO BEAT THE "OFFICE SLUMP"

The quality of work that you turn out depends on your mental and physical fitness for the job, and how you tackle it.

If you are ambitious and conscientious, you are more capable of handling your assignments well, and of being appreciated.

On the other hand, if you are the type who allows herself to become a victim of "office fatigue," you reduce your chances for advancement. Besides, a weary secretary is a hindrance in any office. Not only does she retard progress, but her tired appearance does little to convey a cheerful atmosphere. Below are ten ways to help you beat the "office slump":

1. Eat a nutritious breakfast.

Many people make the mistake of passing up breakfast. After several hours of sleep, your body is without food. Upon rising, a nutritious breakfast is needed to build up an ample reserve of energy. Some workers are satisfied if they just grab a cup of coffee and a doughnut as they dash to the office. By midmorning, they have a definite energy lag which lasts until lunchtime.

2. Avoid eating a heavy lunch.

Eating a heavy meal at lunchtime is not good, either. In addition to causing an uncomfortable feeling, overeating induces drowsiness which will become apparent unless your job commands a great deal of physical activity. Lunching in the office also should be held to a minimum. A midday break *outdoors* gets you into the open and relaxes you so you can accomplish more work in the afternoon.

3. Take a short walk after lunch.

A short walk after lunch is most helpful in aiding digestion and giving your body mild exercise. It is needed by those who sit at desks a good part of the day.

4. Make yourself feel attractive.

Feeling attractive, too, does a great deal toward counteracting fatigue. Special care should be taken regarding your appearance. Refresh your make-up at least once a day, or as often as necessary. Also, a favorite outfit worn on gloomy-weather days perks up your morale.

5. *Avoid feeling gloomy.*

Try always to have a cheerful frame of mind. When you are in good spirits, you will find you can work better.

6. *Check your posture.*

Poor posture can make you feel tired and irritable. Your job requires your working several hours over a typewriter, and you may develop a tendency to slouch and let your head droop forward. Also, your body is not being used sufficiently, and as a consequence, it tires more easily. Below are four ways that will help to relax tired muscles:

  a. Sit erect.

  b. A few times a day stretch your arms and legs.

  c. Don't sit continuously for hours at a time.

  d. Develop the habit of standing while you sort papers, open the mail, file, etc.

7. *Enjoy your work.*

If you feel somewhat burdened and fatigued, try to enjoy the prospects of accomplishment as you are working. By emphasizing the positive aspects, you will get more satisfaction out of your performance.

8. *Alternate hard and easy chores.*

Don't let your job swamp you, either. Plan your work so that you can alternate hard and easy chores. And get it basically organized so that the petty details don't seem too burdensome or monotonous.

9. *Avoid eyestrain.*

Eyestrain, too, makes you cranky and high-strung. If you do work that requires close reading, rest your eyes occasionally during the day. Hints that offer relief for tired eyes are:

  a. Stop what you are doing, close your eyes for a few minutes, then resume your work.

  b. Or, turn to something else that produces less strain on your eyes.

c. Or, walk away from your work for a while. Take a drink of water, sharpen pencils, etc.

10. *Do not keep late hours.*

A schedule of late hours is wearing on your constitution. No matter how physically fit you think you are, your body reaches a breaking point. Don't expect to keep up too active a social schedule and be on the job bright and early to do good work. Your body needs enough rest so it can be sufficiently conditioned for the next day's routine.

You may ask, "How can I perform my responsibilities at the office satisfactorily and still enjoy some social life?"

Here are suggestions that will help to make your workdays more pleasant and productive:

a. Plan your out-of-the-office activities so that they don't interfere with your work. Remember, weekends are best for social functions.

b. As for weekday engagements do not schedule them too close-together. You are likely to find the grind exhausting.

Thus far, considerable emphasis has been placed on the importance of conserving your time and energy in order to avoid fatigue.

The second essential ingredient to top secretarial performance is *working with a system*.

HOW TO WORK WITH A SYSTEM

Let's listen to this conversation between two executives:

"Tell me, Bill," said one executive, "what makes your secretary so competent? She seems to manage all her assignments very skillfully."

"There's nothing so unusual about her," said the other executive, "she just knows how to plan her work."

"Oh, I see," replied the first executive, "she works with a system! You're fortunate to have such an efficient secretary. I wonder if my secretary could be made to realize the importance of working with a system?"

Don't wait until your executive forms doubtful opinions regarding your secretarial ability. Learn, immediately, how to *plan your work*.

A smart secretary learns to organize her tasks to avoid errors. She has a *system* for taking care of details—of checking and double-checking to be certain that nothing is neglected or forgotten or omitted.

The ability to work systematically is attained through proper secretarial training. Education and adaptability are factors which determine how well a secretary is able to perform her duties. In addition, comprehension, retention, intuition, poise, and initiative are all essential qualities that are the basis for outstanding secretarial performance.

If you are the type of secretary who gets frustrated every time you are asked to perform more assignments or more important assignments than you are accustomed to, you are depriving yourself of the pleasures of a richer, more rewarding life. So resolve immediately to turn over a new leaf.

Don't be afraid to do a little more than usual or than is expected of you. You'll be amazed how working with a system will enable you to produce more work, and to produce it more easily and faster. Train yourself to cope with those little "extra duties" today. Tomorrow, you will find you are able to cope with a little more.

With *system* the magic word and the key to top secretarial performance, it is essential that you arrange to take care of the *important chores first*.

For example: Suppose that your executive calls you into his office for dictation. Here are some typical assignments he may ask you to perform:

1. He may dictate several letters to you.

2. He may ask you to type the annual report to be given at a meeting tomorrow.

3. He may give you some correspondence to be filed.

4. He may ask you to type a new organization chart for the department.

5. He may ask you to cancel his luncheon appointment with Mr. Smith which had been set up for today.

6. He may ask you to make plane reservations and other travel arrangements for his trip to the West Coast next week.

After your executive finishes dictating and after you have made notes in your shorthand book of the items that you are to perform, you return to your desk. You sit there, a bit confused, and you may wonder:

"How does he expect me to do all these things! I just can't do them all right away! How can I be sure that I won't forget anything!"

Remember: Remain calm and poised. Think out quietly how you should approach your work.

Two steps must *first* be considered if you are to perform each task accurately and efficiently.

Step 1. Evaluate the importance of each task.

Step 2. Then arrange your tasks in the order in which you will perform them.

For example:

Regarding the dictation: If there is no immediate rush on any of the letters that your executive dictated, you can set aside your shorthand notebook until you have the time to transcribe your shorthand notes. On the other hand, if you are asked to give one or two letters priority over the others, you must be able to fit them into your schedule as soon as convenient. It is important, however, to remember that you have this particular task pending.

Regarding the annual report: There is no immediate rush on this, although it is needed for a meeting tomorrow. You must also fit this item into your schedule as soon as convenient.

Regarding the correspondence to be filed: If you keep a fiile folder on your desk marked "Correspondence To Be Filed," it only takes a second of your time to place the items inside the file folder. This serves as a "temporary file" in which you can keep your unfiled correspondence and other miscellaneous items intact. Then, when time permits, you can file them permanently. Remember, *it is important that your filing be kept up to date.*

Regarding the organization chart for the department: The performance of routine work should be automatic, especially if you know exactly what you must do and how you must do it. The organization chart for the department is somewhat routine in nature. Since there is no immediate rush to complete it, you can set it aside temporarily until you have the time to type it.
Caution: Somehow, routine work is erroneously regarded as unimportant. It is not. Some segments of routine office work. are important and must be completed as soon as convenient.

Regarding the luncheon appointment: The luncheon appointment with Mr. Smith must be cancelled as early in the day as possible. If he is not in his office at the time you call, leave the message with his secretary. By informing Mr. Smith in advance that his luncheon appointment with Mr. Brown is to be cancelled, you will afford him ample time to change his plans for the day. It would be discourteous not to notify him right away. Besides, he would get the impression that your executive was not being polite to him. It is of extreme importance that you *perform this task immediately.*

Regarding the plane reservations: It is important also to make plane reservations and other travel arrangements as soon as possible if your executive is to travel on flights at the times and on the days he designates. So, at your first opportunity, you must see that arrangements for his trip to the West Coast are all set.

Reviewing the above:

Step 1—You have *evaluated the importance of each task.*

Step 2—You have *arranged your tasks in the order in which you will perform them.*

We now come to the next step:

Step 3—The *actual performance.*

Below is the correct order of importance in which the above assignments should be handled. The most urgent task first, the next most urgent task second, and so on.

1. Place the correspondence *to be filed* in the temporary file folder marked "Correspondence To Be Filed."
2. Cancel the luncheon appointment with Mr. Smith.
3. Make plane reservations and other travel arrangements for your executive's trip to the West Coast next week.
4. Transcribe your shorthand notes.
5. Type the annual report to be given at a meeting tomorrow.
6. Type the new organization chart for the department.

Important note: Remember, time is a major factor that is to be considered in the handling of each of the above assignments. In fact, time is an ever important element in accurate and efficient secretarial performance.

PREPARE A PLAN OF PROCEDURE

It is important for you to keep a *plan of procedure* which outlines a step-by-step description of your daily routine. The outline should be easy to follow.

a. It should contain specific instructions on the proper handling of certain chores that it would be difficult for others to understand without such instructions.

b. It should include those items that are detailed and hard

to remember, such as: lists of names, addresses, and the details of other miscellaneous routine chores.

In addition to helping you to increase your skill in your performance, a *plan of procedure* offers the following advantages:

1. If you should be away from the office on vacation, or because of illness, it will prove a valuable aid to the substitute secretary in acquainting her with your duties. Guided by a procedure plan, she will be able to accomplish your work more efficiently and accurately.

2. Also, it will save your executive the trouble of taking time from his busy schedule to explain your specific duties to the temporary secretary.

3. Unnecessary errors or delays will be avoided. Both your responsibilities and your executive's work will be completed properly despite your absence.

KEEPING YOUR DESK NEAT AS YOU WORK

The appearance of your desk is another factor which helps determine how well you handle your assignments. A neat desk, arranged in an orderly fashion, eliminates confusion. Avoid having your desk look like a "rummage bargain counter." Some secretaries just don't care how disorganized their desks look. "I just can't work right unless my desk is cluttered with a lot of papers," they say. "Besides, it makes me look busy!" It is fine to *look busy,* but it isn't necessary to work in this manner to achieve a busy appearance. A disorderly desk only conveys confusion and the impression that you are not able to handle your work as well as you should.

Whenever you have several assignments to perform, remember to handle *one task at a time.* It is a good idea to keep your other assignments in a file folder marked "Pending" on one side of your desk. Put on top of the pile those assignments that require priority. This way, you will be able to complete each task in the order of its importance, faster and more easily.

Regarding other equipment: Your particular attention to the following items will help you to further exhibit your ability and superiority in your job:

1. Objects, such as a calendar, a stapler, a dictionary, and a thesaurus should be neatly arranged *on the top of your desk.*

2. Stationery, envelopes, carbon paper, and telephone message pads (with the exception of one telephone message pad for the current recording of telephone messages) should be kept within easy reach inside your desk.

3. A supply of well-sharpened pencils and other miscellaneous articles (erasers, labels, clips, and rubberbands) should be stored neatly in the sections provided *in the top drawer of your desk.*

You will find that working in an orderly fashion at all times will be to your advantage. You will be regarded by most executives as "the secretary who performs her work at the highest level."

The importance of working systematically cannot be stressed too much. The efficient manner in which you perform your duties is the result of *knowing how to work with a system.*

HOW TO MAKE USE OF YOUR SPARE TIME

A very hard thing for anyone to do is to appear busy when there is nothing to do. This can present a serious problem.

Some secretaries, to look busy, think they are solving the situation if they read a book or a magazine during slack periods. This is wrong. It only proves two things:

1. That your executive doesn't have enough work to give you.

2. That you aren't capable of handling very many responsibilities.

Remember, the secretary is under constant scrutiny and so she is an easy target for criticism.

Ponder this:

As a good secretary, you constantly have to prove your worth. Rather than sit idle or read magazines, take advantage of any slack periods by learning more about the business. There are a number of things you can take care of when you have no particular chore to perform. Here are some examples:

1. Complete items you did not find time to take care of when you were busy.
2. Requisition office supplies, such as carbon paper, letterheads, pencils, and the like.
3. Read through the files to get a better understanding of the work.
4. If you find that some file folders are old and worn, replace them with new file folders.
5. Weed out unnecessary correspondence from files that have become thick and cumbersome.

It is even possible that while you are delving in the files, you may find an important letter or document that has been missing for some time.

Your ability to initiate action, even in small ways, will be greatly appreciated. Most executives prefer their secretaries to do things without being told.

SUMMARY OF 18 WAYS TO AVOID OFFICE FATIGUE

For your convenience, the 18 ways to avoid fatigue are summarized below:

1. Plan your work for the day.
2. Know what is important and what is not important.
3. Develop a good memory.
4. Use proper work tools.
5. Assemble the next day's assignments the day before.
6. Handle one task at a time.
7. Listen carefully to instructions.
8. Carry out instructions exactly as they have been given.
9. Eat a nutritious breakfast.
10. Avoid eating a heavy lunch.
11. Take a short walk after lunch.
12. Make yourself feel attractive.
13. Avoid feeling gloomy.
14. Check your posture.
15. Enjoy your work.
16. Alternate hard and easy chores.
17. Avoid eyestrain.
18. Do not keep late hours.

Chapter 4

EXTENDING SERVICE

WITH A SMILE

PROPER HANDLING OF THE TELEPHONE

Ask any efficient secretary what she thinks is the most important instrument in the business office and almost without exception she will reply . . . "The telephone."

Question: Why is the telephone regarded as such an important business instrument?

Answer: Because the telephone provides communication by voice, the pleasing tone of your voice is a primary requirement in making friends and creating good will.

Remember, the impression that you make on the telephone is just as important as the one you make in person.

You might ask: "How should my voice sound if I want to make a good impression?"

Answer: "It should be no different than when you are conversing with someone face to face."

83

Answering the telephone

A pleasant voice, tact, and quickness of wit are the main qualifications that are needed in the proper handling of the telephone.

The favorable impression that is made on the caller by a clear, clean-cut voice, restrained, and of pleasing tone cannot be overestimated.

As a secretary, you should try to cultivate such a manner of speaking over the telephone, if you do not already possess it. Be especially careful of the inflection of your voice. A pleasant voice, "the voice with a smile," is of the greatest value in telephoning. Don't make the mistake of trying to show how businesslike you are by speaking curtly or snappishly.

Here are two easy methods by which you can develop a good telephone personality:

1. Be courteous.
2. Speak gently, distinctly, and *slowly*.

During the course of your workday, you are required to answer the telephone any number of times. Since your *voice* indicates both your personality and your attitude toward the caller, proper handling of the telephone is *essential*.

The following are good telephone rules to follow:

1. First of all, be *prompt* in answering the telephone. (Caution: The caller should not be kept waiting. Some secretaries let the telephone ring two or three times before they turn to answer it. Such a practice can destroy the good will of the caller. As a secretary, you are an ambassador of good will, and it is up to you to treat the person calling with the *utmost* courtesy.)

2. Your mood and attitude should be cheerful.

3. Talk directly into the mouthpiece.

4. In a quiet, well-modulated voice, express your words and ideas clearly and distinctly.

5. Be courteous and as brief as possible without appearing unfriendly.

6. Listen attentively to avoid the necessity of having to ask the caller to repeat.

7. When you have completed your conversation, replace the phone on the receiver *gently*. No one likes to have the phone slammed in his ear.

Proper application of the above points to each telephone call will help to *improve your service.*

IDENTIFYING YOURSELF ON THE TELEPHONE

The combination of a friendly manner and a business-like approach will make identifying yourself on the telephone a pleasant task.

Remember, what you say and how you say it, gives the person calling either a good or a bad impression of you and your company.

When you answer the telephone, don't use time-consuming words such as "Hello" and "Yes?" The best way to answer is to identify yourself by announcing your name. For example: "Miss Reade."

If you work in a particular department, announce both your department and your name. For example: "Purchasing Department, Miss Reade."

By the tone of these few words of identification, you can convey a friendly welcome which will imply your willingness to be helpful. In fact, the cordial interest that you create in all your telephone conversations enables the caller to converse without having to answer annoying questions such as "Who's speaking?" or "What department do you represent?"

Recording a message

When a message is to be left, (1) Get it quickly and correctly, (2) be sure you have the correct spelling of the caller's name, (3) use the Telephone Message form provided to record the details of the message as given by the caller.

Below is a form which suggests the necessary items for recording a complete message:

```
For         Mr. Brown

From        Mr. Smith

Of          Smith & Company

Phone No.   EX 8-0000              Ext. 405

Telephoned          (x)  Will Call You Later (‾)

Please Call         (‾)  Came To See You      (‾)

Returned Your Call (‾)  Wishes To See You    (‾)

                    MESSAGE

    Asked if you will be able to attend a
    luncheon meeting at the Businessmen's
    Club on Thursday, May 11, at 12:15 P.M.




                 Miss
    Rec'd By Reade    Date  5/1    Time 10:15 A.M.
```

In writing down the details of a message, the following steps should be observed:

Step 1: Ask for the caller's name and telephone number. Telephone messages are recorded so that the person to whom the call was made can return the call. Therefore, if you don't already know the caller's name and telephone number, you are required to ask him.

To avoid offending the person calling, *request* the information that you need, rather than demanding it. Use expressions such as: "May I have your name?" instead of, "What's your name?" "Does Mr. Brown have your telephone number?" instead of "What's your number?"

Step 2: For the spelling of difficult names, it is helpful if you use key words to distinguish letters that sound alike on the telephone. For example: "A, as in Alice," "B, as in Bertha," etc.

The following *key words* are suggested:

A—Alice	J—James	S—Samuel
B—Bertha	K—Kate	T—Thomas
C—Charles	L—Lewis	U—Utah
D—David	M—Mary	V—Victor
E—Edward	N—Nellie	W—William
F—Frank	O—Oliver	X—X-Ray
G—George	P—Peter	Y—Young
H—Henry	Q—Quaker	Z—Zebra
I—Ida	R—Robert	

Step 3: To avoid the possibility of error or misunderstanding *read back* all messages to the person who is calling.

The most important items to be repeated are:
1. The caller's name.
2. The caller's telephone number and extension.
3. If a date is set, repeat the day, the time, and the place on which the meeting will take place.

As a final thought on the subject of recording telephone messages, when you write down a message that the wife of your executive called, the tone of such phrases as: *"Call your wife"* or *"Your wife telephoned"* sounds rather discourteous. It is true that she is his wife, but there is a better way to refer to her in business. *"Mrs. Brown asks you to call her"* or *"Mrs. Brown telephoned"* are more respectful.

INTERCEPTING TELEPHONE CALLS

There are times when the secretary is called upon to screen her executive's telephone calls. Utmost tact and common sense are needed in handling the situation.

There are three *musts* when you are intercepting telephone calls:

1. You must be able to determine the identity of the caller without appearing inquisitive.
2. You must avoid giving an impression of discrimination.
3. You must make the caller feel that you are willing to serve him.

To eliminate the use of the phrase "Who's calling?" which sounds rather abrupt, other phrases can be used effectively, without creating resentment.

Let's assume that you are secretary to Mr. William E. Brown, Sales Promotion Manager with the Jaymar Construction Company. The following are a few model telephone conversations which show how various callers are to be handled. These should serve to indicate how you can best handle each situation that arises.

SITUATION: Suppose Mr. Brown is out of the office when his telephone rings:

Example 1.
Secretary: "Mr. Brown's office, Miss Reade."

Caller: "Is Mr. Brown available?"
Secretary: "Mr. Brown is not available at the moment; may I tell him who called?"
Caller: "My name is Mr. Deal. Will you have Mr. Brown call me please? My telephone number is 000-000."

Example 2.
Secretary: "Mr. Brown's office, Miss Reade."
Caller: "Is Mr. Brown there?"
Secretary: "Mr. Brown is not in his office at the moment; may I take a message?"
Caller: "No message, thank you. Just tell him that I called. This is Mr. Johnson. My telephone number is 000-0000."

Example 3.
Secretary: "Mr. Brown's office, Miss Reade."
Caller: "Is he there?" (Voice deep and authoritative)
Secretary: "Mr. Brown is not in his office. Is there something I can do?"
Caller: "Yes, have him call me as soon as possible . . . Mr. Jones." (A strong emphasis on his name)
(Note: Mr. Jones is the Treasurer of your organization.)
Secretary: "Yes, Mr. Jones, I'll have Mr. Brown call you as soon as he returns."

Example 4.
Secretary: "Mr. Brown's office, Miss Reade."
Caller: "May I speak to Mr. Brown?"
Secretary: "Mr. Brown is not at his desk just now. If you will leave your name and telephone number, I will have him call you."
Caller: "My name is Mr. Roger Jamison. I can be reached at 000-0000."

Example 5.
Secretary: "Mr. Brown's office, Miss Reade."
Caller: "Mr. Brown, please."

Secretary: "Mr. Brown is out of the office. He will not be back until this afternoon; may I have him call you?"
Caller: "Yes, when he gets a chance. This is Mr. Havemeyer."

SITUATION: Suppose Mr. Brown is on another telephone:
Secretary: "Mr. Brown is talking on another phone; will you wait a moment?"
Caller: (He will either say that he will wait or ask to have Mr. Brown call him back.)

SITUATION: Suppose Mr. Brown is attending a meeting:
Secretary: "Mr. Brown is attending a meeting; may I have him call you when he returns?"
Caller: (He most likely will ask to have Mr. Brown return his call.)

Sometimes specific situations arise which require special handling and utmost tact.

SITUATION: Occasionally your executive will accept calls but wishes to know the name of the person calling.
You might say: "May I tell Mr. Brown who's calling, please?"

SITUATION: If Mr. Brown wishes to be available to certain callers, it might be preferable to say:
"Mr. Brown is not available at the moment. May I have him call you?"

SITUATION: Perhaps the caller is someone with whom Mr. Brown will talk; he can then be connected by saying:
"Here is Mr. Brown now" or "I'll see if I can get Mr. Brown for you, Mr. Smith."

ANSWERING PHONES OF OTHERS IN THE OFFICE

If you are employed in a large organization, or in a department where there are several telephones that are used by the others in your office, you are expected to answer their phones when they are left unattended. To let the phones ring unanswered gives a bad impression.

Remember, you don't know who is calling. It may be one of the company's best clients, a prospective client, a good friend, or a top official of the company. You will want to make sure the person calling feels he is being greeted in a friendly fashion. The promptness and pleasantness of your answer often determine the reaction of the caller. This is good public relations.

A pleasing voice and a cordial manner are important business assets which will encourage a spirit of friendliness within and toward your organization. So, the next time the other person's phone rings, answer it promptly.

A word of advice: It is wise to find out who is calling. If the caller does not identify himself, the phrase "May I tell Mr. Blank who is calling?" will help to get results.

SITUATION: Sometimes the person called may be out of his office or away from his desk and you don't know where he is.

To say: "Mr. Blank is not here" makes the caller think Mr. Blank purposely left the office to avoid speaking with him.

Instead, you should say: "Mr. Blank stepped out of the office for a moment. May I have him call you?" implying that Mr. Blank is willing to speak with the caller.

SITUATION: Often the other person called may be on another extension.

Don't say: "Mr. Blank is busy right now."

It is best to say: "I'm sorry, but Mr. Blank is talking on another phone. May I take a message for him?"

This method indicates your willingness to serve.

Two important points to remember:

1. When you take a message for the other person in your office, be sure that you write it down clearly so that he can understand it. Then leave it where he will see it, preferably on his desk.

2. When you answer the other person's phone, don't say: "Mr. Blank's wire."

The use of the word *wire* gives the impression that the caller is speaking to an inanimate object.

Say instead: "Mr. Blank's extension" or "Mr. Blank's office" to convey a spirit of friendliness.

Transferring telephone calls

When it is necessary to transfer a call to another telephone, you must explain the reason to the caller. It may be that the person calling wants to speak with someone in another department. The best way to handle this is to say:

"I'm sorry, you have the wrong extension; you want Mr. Norton in the Order Department. One moment, please, I'll have you transferred."

If the caller accepts your offer to transfer him, then you should signal the switchboard attendant *slowly* to get her attention.

(Caution: Do not jiggle the signal button—but push *down* and *up* to a *one* (pause) *two* beat. Too fast pushing will disconnect the caller.)

When you get the switchboard attendant, you should say: "Will you transfer this call to Mr. Norton in the Order Department?" (or use extension number, if known).

Or you can say: "This call is for Mr. Norton in the Order Department. Will you please transfer this call to extension (mention extension number)."

Wait for the attendant's reply to make sure she understands you. Only then, replace the phone.

PLACING TELEPHONE CALLS

The chore of placing calls is rather simple.

First of all, be sure you have the correct telephone number.

Secondly, dial correctly. Nobody likes wrong numbers. If you reach the wrong number, it is courteous to say simply, "I'm sorry. I dialed incorrectly."

Thirdly, pronounce names and telephone numbers distinctly.

TERMINATING TELEPHONE CALLS

In terminating calls, it is desirable to end each conversation in a friendly, unhurried manner that will give the person calling the impression that you are glad to have had the opportunity of serving him. Be sure, however, that you wait for the caller to say "Good-bye." He may have an afterthought and he will be annoyed if you hang up too soon.

A word of advice: Your success in handling the telephone depends largely upon thoughtful effort and common sense. Just keep in mind that good manners are even more essential over the telephone than in face-to-face conversations. A mistake in talking directly to a person on a face-to-face basis can be easily corrected but there is no opportunity to correct a lack of courtesy over the telephone.

Some secretaries are merely marking time in their profession because they haven't bothered to prepare themselves for going further. Somebody better qualified is always sure to get ahead of them.

Don't let this happen to you. There is absolutely no reason why you can't handle your telephone properly. Think about extending "service with a smile" and putting it to work effectively every time you make or answer a call.

Meriting good will and having people enjoy telephoning you are largely a matter of dealing with others as you would have them deal with you.

A good telephone personality is the result of:

—learning HOW TO ANSWER THE TELEPHONE.
—learning HOW TO IDENTIFY YOURSELF ON THE TELEPHONE.
—learning HOW TO RECORD A MESSAGE.
—learning HOW TO INTERCEPT TELEPHONE CALLS.
—learning HOW TO ANSWER THE OTHER PERSON'S TELEPHONE.
—learning HOW TO TRANSFER TELEPHONE CALLS.
—learning HOW TO PLACE TELEPHONE CALLS.
—learning HOW TO TERMINATE TELEPHONE CALLS.

HOW TO RECEIVE VISITORS TO THE OFFICE

In a busy office the secretary must take care of at least half of the callers who come to see her executive. And here nothing makes her more effective than a friendly, gracious manner.

Five essential ingredients of this effectiveness are: (1) poise, (2) harmony, (3) friendliness, (4) good manners, and (5) a pleasing voice.

All these basic qualities form the foundation for creating good will and winning friends. More important, they help to make you a gracious, magnetic, and agreeable individual.

When you meet a caller face to face, the pleasantness of your first greeting makes a good impression. It is an indication that you want to make him feel he is welcome.

Using good manners

Perhaps the visitor is a prospective customer, a salesman, a client, a friend or acquaintance: The best way you can assure an agreeable tone to the interview is to be friendly, courteous, and interested.

1. If you are *friendly,* you make the visitor feel at ease.
2. If you are *courteous,* you show you have consideration for his feelings.

3. If you are *interested,* you encourage him to talk.

Good manners and consideration for the feelings of others are priceless business as well as social assets.

Expressions such as "Thank you," "I'm sorry," and "I beg your pardon" are essentials in the art of making a good impression. So are letting the other person finish what he has to say without interruption and avoiding any signs of impatience.

Remembering certain facts about the caller is also helpful. Usually people like to be addressed by their names, together with their titles when appropriate. Examples of such courtesy, which pleases the caller, are as follows:

"Mr. Brown will see you now, *Mr. Jones,* or *Mrs. Jones,* or *Miss Jones.*"

Perhaps the caller is a doctor of medicine or a holder of degrees:

"Mr. Brown will be with you momentarily, *Dr. Wharton.* Won't you please sit down and make yourself comfortable?"

Or perhaps the caller is a member of the clergy:

"Mr. Brown is rather busy just now, *Reverend O'Connell* or *Rabbi Kronish.* Is there something I can do for you?"

Or perhaps the caller is in a branch of the services:

"Good morning, *Colonel Compton* or *Lieutenant Compton.* Mr. Brown is away from his desk at the moment. As soon as he returns, I shall tell him you are here."

HAVING A PLEASING VOICE

Your manner of speech also plays an essential role in whether you create a good or a bad impression. A pleasant speaking voice, both on the telephone and with callers, is a great asset.

In greeting people for the first time, it should be remembered, it isn't only *what* you say, but *how* you say it that often makes the person want to come back again.

Three characteristics should help you to attain poise, self-confidence, and a more pleasing personality. They are:

1. *Voice quality.* Your voice should be pleasant, neither too loud nor too soft, neither too high nor too low.
2. *Distinct articulation.* You should speak clearly.
3. *Clear enunciation.* You should enunciate each syllable distinctly.

Using tact

Because every caller feels that his reason for visiting is important, it is essential that he be handled tactfully.

As an office receptionist for your executive, you should not strive to get rid of visitors, with flat refusals, but, instead, you should try to give them *two* impressions: (1) that they have been treated courteously; and (2) that they have accomplished with you as much as they would have accomplished with your executive.

To give callers these two impressions, (a) you should be courteous, interested, and sympathetic; also (b) you should strive to please and to do as much as possible for the caller.

Classifying callers

You must develop the ability to classify callers according to the importance of their business. Callers come under *three* different classifications.

You must be quick to judge:

—which callers are welcome, so that you can prevent the callers whom your executive is not desirous of seeing from taking up his valuable time;

—which callers should be seen by someone else in the organization; and

—which callers you should take care of yourself.

OBTAINING FACTS ABOUT THE CALLER

Knowing your executive's needs and desires, you should be able to ascertain *three* facts about every caller:

1. *The name of the caller*

There are two main reasons for getting the name of the caller. Firstly, you should know to whom you are talking and what consideration is to be given to that particular caller. Secondly, there may be certain persons your executive does not want to see.

2. *The caller's business*

The reason for ascertaining the business of the caller is this: You are the one to decide if the caller's business is important enough for your executive's consideration.

3. *The nature of the caller's visit*

After learning what brought the caller to his office, your executive should be better prepared to meet the caller and discuss the nature of his errand more intelligently.

SUMMING UP

Alertness, patience, and a desire to do all you can for the caller are required.

1. Sympathize with the caller by showing regret if you have to refuse his request to see your executive.

2. If the caller wishes to talk with you, be courteous and keep the conversation general.

3. In cases where the caller is so persistent that he will not accept your explanations, ask him to send a letter to your executive asking for an appointment.

4. If you are employed in a large organization where the caller is greeted by a receptionist, and your executive is ready to see him, you should see that he is escorted to your executive's office. Do not allow him to *wander around unescorted.*

5. Be ready to perform any special services which your executive may ask you to do for the caller, such as getting information, taking dictation, obtaining theatre tickets, making hotel or travel reservations, and the like.

6. After the meeting, expressions, such as "Good-bye, Mr. Jones, it was good to see you again" or "I hope you will visit us again, soon" should send the caller off smiling.

When you have mastered the necessary details in handling callers, you will be surprised at the ease with which you get visitors to confide in you.

Experience and a pleasant manner will soon make you proficient in handling callers, both on the telephone and face to face. This special proficiency, of course, is the result of extending "service with a smile."

Chapter 5

HOW TO IMPROVE

YOUR TYPING SKILL

If secretaries were asked: "What office device do you think secretaries consider most helpful in the office, the majority of them would agree, "The typewriter."

The typewriter has added enormously to the usefulness of the secretary and has helped her to be an efficient worker in the business office.

1. It enables her to turn out work more quickly and with greater ease.

2. It provides a *more* legible copy than script.

3. It makes several copies of carbon duplicates at the same time that the original is written.

These are just a few of the many reasons why *typing is a most vital skill in the business world.*

As a secretary, *your* job calls for you to type great numbers of letters and reports every day. The volume of your work requires fast, accurate typewriting skill which can be developed *only* with adequate practice.

If you follow all the basic rules of typing, you can become an efficient typist.

Whether you are an electric typist or a manual typist, you will want to heed the following hints:

1. KNOW YOUR TYPEWRITER

First of all, you must know your typewriter in detail. A thorough knowledge of the keyboard is essential. In learning the keyboard, three elements are involved: (1) letters, (2) fingers, and (3) keys.

Letters. You must know what letters each finger strikes and where each letter is located. *Fingers.* Your fingers must be kept set on the "home keys" before you begin typing. In the case of an electric typewriter, since the slightest pressure can activate typing, it is advisable to just hover your fingers lightly over the "home keys." *Keys.* As you type, strike each key with a light, quick stroke. Do not press the keys, but "tap" them sharply.

Secondly, you must know all the operating parts of your typewriter and their use.

Thirdly, you must have sufficient practice to operate each part of the machine *instinctively,* that is, automatically, without thinking.

2. CORRECT TYPING POSTURE

An essential to good typing practice is correct posture. It is absolutely necessary for achieving more efficient typing results.

Unfortunately, some secretaries fail to recognize the importance of posture. Correct posture has advantages: Besides enabling you to be comfortable while you are typing, correct posture helps to offset fatigue. Fatigue is a major problem among many typists. This is because fatigue leads to mistakes, typographical or otherwise.

When you work several hours continuously at your typewriter, you will begin to feel a definite energy lag. Although you may be impelled to complete your work, you can't reduce fatigue simply by continuing the activity in which you are engaged.

Tension induces fatigue. So you must learn how to *relax* at your work during the day.

A moment to sit "tall" and to stand "tall" will help you to increase your work output.

A few minutes away from your desk will help to ease tension.

A change of tasks also will help to ward off fatigue. Of course, if you have a typing chore that has to be done at a certain time, you *must* stay with it until it is finished.

To obtain satisfactory results and to keep from getting tense, try to approach your work in a calm manner. Once you have become relaxed, stay relaxed.

The following *Do's* for *correct typing posture* should help you to improve your skill in *electric typing* or in *manual typing*.

ELECTRIC TYPING DO'S

1. Place your "work" that is to be typed at either the right or left side of your typewriter—preferably the right side, if this is convenient.

2. When you start typing, begin slowly.

3. Keep your fingertips close to the keys in a natural, curved position.

4. Tap the keys squarely in their centers, using a quick, sharp touch.

5. Relax finger pressure the instant you contact the keys.

6. Keep your upper arms sloped slightly forward.

7. Your forearms should be on the same slope as keyboard.

8. Sit erect but relaxed, with your back supported by the chair backrest.

9. Keep feet flat on the floor.

MANUAL TYPING DO'S

1. Place your "work" that is to be typed at either the right or left side of your typewriter—preferably the right side, if this is convenient.

2. Curve your fingers so that you strike each key sharply, letting them rest lightly on the "guide keys" and your right thumb on the space bar.

3. Let your wrists slant slightly downward, and relax them completely.

4. Keep your forearms relaxed and in a horizontal position.

5. Hold your elbows motionless.

6. Sit erect but relaxed, with your body leaning slightly forward.

7. Keep your feet flat on the floor with one foot slightly ahead of the other for better balance.

8. Hold your head erect and your eyes focused on your work.

3. PROPER HANDLING OF PAPER

Before typing has begun, there are a few points regarding the handling of paper that need careful attention. They are:

INSERTING THE SHEET OF PAPER

To insert the paper with complete accuracy, rest the sheet squarely on the paper table and against the paper guide. Turn the platen or "roller" and give it a quick twist.

STRAIGHTENING THE SHEET OF PAPER

For neat, attractive work, your paper must not slant in the machine. As you turn the platen, watch for the appearance of the top edge of the sheet and see that it is parallel with the line scale. If it is not, press the paper release lever and straighten the edge of the sheet. Then return the lever to its original position.

SETTING MARGINAL STOPS

For neatness, regulate the width of the left-hand and right-hand margins so that your typewritten work is evenly centered on the sheet of paper.

INSERTING CARBON PAPER

There are different ways of inserting carbon paper between several sheets of paper. Following are *two* methods frequently used by many secretaries.

Problem: Suppose you need an original and three carbon copies. Total quantity—*four sheets* of paper.

Here is the first method:

Method No. 1

Step 1: (First Sheet) Hold the first sheet of paper in your left hand.

Step 2: (Carbon) With your right hand, place a carbon, *carbon side downward,* directly behind the first sheet of paper which you have in your left hand.

Step 3: (Second Sheet) Again with the right hand, place the second sheet of paper directly behind the first carbon.

Step 4: (Carbon) Then, take the second carbon, *carbon side downward,* and place it directly behind the second sheet of paper.

Step 5: (Third Sheet) Take the third sheet of paper and place it directly behind the second carbon.

Step 6: (Carbon) Then, take the third carbon, *carbon side downward,* and place it directly behind the third sheet of paper.

Step 7: (Fourth Sheet) Take the fourth sheet of paper and place it directly behind the third and last carbon.

Result: One complete carbon pack.

Note: Remember to straighten the top edge of the sheets of paper and the carbons contained in the carbon pack before you insert them into the typewriter.

A helpful suggestion: Some secretaries, after straightening the carbon pack, place an envelope with an open flap along the top edge. When the flap is closed and the pack is fed into the typewriter, it feeds through straight.

The second method is this:

Method No. 2

Step 1: Straighten the four sheets of paper and insert the top edge into the typewriter so that the sheets are held firmly by the master feed roll of the typewriter.

Step 2: Place one carbon, *carbon side upward,* between the first sheet and the second sheet of paper.

Step 3: Place the second carbon, *carbon side upward,* between the second sheet and the third sheet of paper.

Step 4: Place the third carbon, *carbon side upward,* between the third sheet and the fourth sheet of paper.

Step 5: Next, roll the carbon pack containing the four sheets of paper and the carbons into the typewriter. If they are not parallel with the line scale, press the paper release lever to release the carbon pack for straightening. Then return the lever to its original position.

Step 6: Roll out the carbon pack to a designated point for typing. Set the marginal stops, and begin to type.

A helpful suggestion: In counting out the carbons that you need, remember to count *one carbon less* than the number of sheets. For example: If you have 6 sheets of paper, count out 5 carbons. For 4 sheets of paper, count out 3 carbons, and so on.

Most typists prefer to use the first method. However, the second method is simpler. Less time is consumed in placing the carbons between the sheets of paper. Use whichever method you find is most convenient.

An even faster method involves the use of carbon sets that come with the carbon paper already inserted between the sheets. Because carbon sets completely eliminate the handling of carbon paper, they are playing an increasingly important role in aiding the secretary to turn out a quantity of work with a minimum amount of effort.

REMOVING THE SHEET OF PAPER

When you take the paper out of the typewriter, press the paper release lever with one hand. Grasp the paper in the middle at the top and pull it out. Remember, never pull the paper out without first pressing the paper release lever. You might loosen the platen grip in the carriage. You might even tear the paper on which you have just typed your work.

4. HOW TO DEVELOP TYPING SKILL

Like every secretary, you will want a typewriter that leaves you feeling fresh at the end of the day. It takes proper training and *typing skill* to acquire expert control of your typewriter so that it will enable you to turn out better-looking work, more easily, and faster.

The first and most important element of typing skill is *accuracy*. Without accuracy, typing is worthless.

1. ACCURACY

Three essentials to accuracy are: (a) concentration; (b) keeping your eyes on the copy; and (c) elimination of unnecessary motions.

Concentration is very important in developing typing skill. If you do not give conscientious attention to the task you are performing, you *will* make mistakes. Too many errors mean more retyping, rush, and sometimes, after-hours of work. For accurate typing performance, it is an advantage if you do the following:

a. Concentrate *only* on the task you are performing.
b. Become oblivious to everything *except* your typing.
c. If possible, read a word or more ahead of what you are typing.

Keeping your eyes on the copy means exactly that. It is a *must* if you are to acquire speed and accuracy. Looking back and forth from copy to typewriter, and from typewriter to copy causes a break in your line of vision. This means loss of time and speed. In addition, there is the possibility that you might type a wrong word. You might even skip a sentence, or even a paragraph. To avoid making such errors, it is wise to set the copy you are typing at an angle and in the *best position* so that you can read it easily and without strain.

Elimination of unnecessary motions is another essential to accuracy. There seems to be a tendency among some typists, and among beginners especially, to move their hands up and down unnecessarily as they strike each key. Such motions are tiring and time-consuming. After each key is struck quickly and sharply, go immediately to the next key as you hold your hands over the "guide keys"—and keep on typing at a steady pace.

2. RHYTHM

In typing, *rhythm* means a smooth continuity of typing, that is, a natural continuous pace over a period of time at a steady rate of speed.

There can be no satisfactory results unless a rhythmic stroke is developed. A rhythmic stroke means more than just attaining a regular beat. It means: (1) hitting each key with a quick, sharp blow, and (2) hitting each key with equal force.

Regarding electric typing. Rhythm seems to be less important in electric typing than in manual typing. Your stroke takes no pressure at all. You merely use a "tap" stroke with a relaxed, tension-free movement.

Some electric typewriters are equipped with a new feature designed to guarantee every typist maximum quality work regardless of her touch. Simply by moving the touch control lever, you can personalize the "electric touch" to match your individual typing stroke without affecting the quality of the typed impression.

Regarding manual typing. For smoother typing, the following method will enable you to reach an accelerated rate of speed until the maximum speed of which you are capable is reached.

When you type, begin slowly as you spell out each word in the sentence silently. Then, gradually increase your speed of spelling as you go along. For example:

Suppose that you are typing this sentence: *Real skill is the sure reward of purposeful effort.*

With your fingers set on the "guide keys" you begin to type as you say each letter to yourself.

EXAMPLE: REAL (Space) SKILL (Space) IS (Space) THE (Space) SURE (Space) REWARD (Space) OF (Space) PURPOSEFUL (Space) EFFORT (Period)

It is surprising how your typing speed increases automatically, as your fingers strike each key, according to the rhythm of your spelling.

Note: Once you have attained a rhythmic stroke, it won't be necessary, then, to spell any further. However, if you feel that you are typing in spurts, it is wise to spell out a few words occasionally at various intervals so you can maintain an even rate of speed from start to finish.

3. Speed

Most electric typewriters have a controlled speed action which guarantees every typist the maximum speed for satisfactory typing performance.

However, if you are to maintain a uniform rate of speed and to gain the skill which is needed for accurate typing performance, the following rules can be applied to either electric or manual typing.

1. Smoothness, *first*.
2. Then, type as fast you can accurately.
3. There should be no breaks in your typing.
4. Strive for a natural continuous stroke.
5. Slow down if necessary to maintain an even rate of speed.

Here is a special note regarding typing in general: It is more important for you to type accurately than to type rapidly. *Accuracy cannot be overemphasized,* as accuracy is the foundation upon which speed must be developed.

Thus far, considerable emphasis has been placed on the importance of speed and accuracy—the *two* basic elements of typing skill.

You may not believe it, but *making clean, neat corrections* on your typewritten work is another essential of typing skill. In fact, it is an *art*.

5. HOW TO MAKE CORRECTIONS

Some secretaries regard erasing as a difficult task. Actually, it is quite simple once you've acquired skill and practice.

Letters that have noticeable erasures should be retyped. However, if you *must* make a correction, don't let a careless erasure spoil the appearance of your typewritten work. It is of the greatest importance to have your letters "look" neat.

A word of caution: Erasures in vital information such as prices, dimensions, and sums of money are *never* permitted.

ERASING ORIGINAL AND CARBONS WHILE COPY IS IN THE TYPEWRITER

Corrections are made on the carbons as well as the original. This is *essential* if the carbon copies are to contain the exact information as the original.

Below are *four* easy steps that should help to make carbon correcting a not unpleasant chore.

Step 1: First, insert a card or a piece of paper in front of each carbon at the point of correction.

Step 2: Then, to prevent smudges on the original copy, use a hard eraser. For best results in erasing, use a light stroke horizontally.

Step 3: Next, use a gum or soft eraser for the carbons. To prevent smudging, place a piece of paper above the carbon sheet and hold one finger on the piece of paper to avoid slipping.

Step 4: Finally, remove the card or paper which you placed in front of the carbons and type in the correct letter or word.

An important note: The following suggestions are recommended when you are making corrections.

1. To avoid erasing additional material, a celluloid or steel shield with an opening of proper size will help you in erasing individual letters or words.

2. Erased spots may be cleaned with a bit of white chalk rubbed on lightly and then dusted off.

3. Impressions of letters that are still visible can be cleaned with a razor blade by scraping lightly over the typed surface.

4. When you use KO-REC-TYPE to make a correction, be sure that the correction is made on the carbons, as well as the original. Some secretaries tend to disregard correcting the carbons. As a result, the carbons are left with strikeovers. The disadvantage here is that, in the case of figures, a strikeover can cause confusion as to which figure is correct. Also, if a photocopy is made of the carbon, as is necessary at times, the error will show up on the copy.

Filling-in

When re-inserting the typewritten sheet into the machine to make the fill-in, the following method will prove helpful:

Step 1: Align such letters as "l" or "i" with the vertical white lines on the line scale.

Step 2: Use the paper release lever and the variable line spacer to make the alignment.

Step 3: Before you type in the correct letter, tap the key lightly to determine whether the alignment is absolutely correct.

Spacing on the typewriter

If your typewriter has a proportional spacing attachment, you will be able to insert a letter which has been omitted, or remove a letter which has been added. You can easily erase the entire word and retype the spacing to fit.

If your typewriter does not have a half-spacing attachment, the following examples will help you to achieve the same good results:

1. INSERTING A LETTER

Suppose that you are inserting a letter at the beginning or the end of a word.

Manual Typing. You simply press the backspacer lightly so that the carriage is moved slightly away from the typed letter. Then, tap the key of the letter that is to be added lightly for proper alignment and type in the correct letter.

Electric Typing. Since the backspacer on the electric typewriter does not move slightly away from the typed letter as it does on the manual typewriter, you simply move the carriage with your left hand slightly away from the typed letter. Hold it firm with your hand in the desired typing position. Then, lightly tap the key of the letter that is to be added for proper alignment, and type in the correct letter.

An easier way to get the proper alignment of the letter that is to be added is this: On some electric typewriters you simply press the ribbon control lever down for stencil position. On others, it is the stencil button. Then, tap the key lightly, and only a stenciled impression of the letter is shown, rather than a typewritten letter. If the impression indicates that the letter is in proper alignment, then, return the ribbon control lever or the stencil button to writing position and type in the letter that is to be added.

2. REMOVING A LETTER

Removing a letter is just as simple. First, erase the letter that is to be omitted. If it is at the beginning or the end of the word, less effort is required in concealing the omission.

If you are removing an extra letter that was accidentally typed in the middle of the word, you simply erase one or two letters on either side of the letter that is to be omitted.

Note 1. If you are using a *manual typewriter,* here is how it is done: As you backspace and lightly tap the keys for proper alignment, you retype the spacing to fit.

Note 2. If the correction is being made on an *electric typewriter,* you simply move the carriage either to the left or the right for proper alignment, and retype the spacing to fit.

6. TYPING SHORTCUTS

Outlined below are ten shortcuts that will enable you to produce the best work with the least amount of effort.

1. HOW TO FIND THE CENTER OF THE SHEET

There are three ways of finding the center of the sheet. The first method is as follows:

Step 1: Insert the paper with the left edge at 0.

Step 2: Then, take the scale reading at the right edge and divide by two to find the center number. For example: Suppose the scale reading indicates the total number of spaces across the width of the paper to be 60. Divide by two and you get 30, which is the center of the sheet. See diagram below:

	Center	
0	30	60

The second method is this:

Step 1: Take another sheet of paper the same size as the one that is to be used for typing, fold it over in the middle.

Step 2: Align the top edges of both sheets, and keep the one for typing underneath.

Step 3: At the top edge of the folded sheet, make a light pencil dot on the underneath sheet to mark the center. See diagram below:

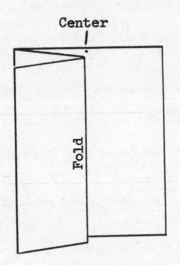

The third method:

This can be done on some *electric typewriters* that have a Clear View Card Holder which is described below:

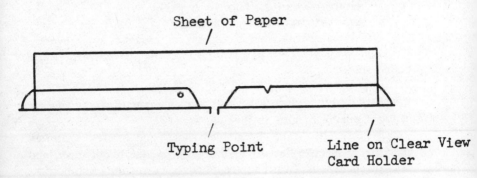

After you have the paper set in the typewriter for typing, adjust the left- and right-hand edges of the paper for proper alignment with the lines indicated on the left and right edges of the Clear View Card Holder. When the alignment is made, immediately the typing point becomes the center of the sheet.

Note: This can be done *only* with the 8½ x 11 inches sheet of paper.

2. How to center the title or subhead

Centering the title or heading is rather simple.

Step 1: From the *center* point of the sheet, backspace *once* for every *two* letters as follows:

Suppose you are centering this heading: Typing Your Way Upward

Example: As you backspace, say to yourself: TY/PI/NG/ Space Y/OU/R Space/WA/Y Space/UP/WA/RD

Step 2: Then, at the last backspacing point, type in the heading—and *presto,* the heading is evenly centered on the page.

3. How to correct pages
stapled together at the top

Following are two simple steps for making corrections on bound sheets:

Step 1: First, place a blank sheet of paper in the typewriter in the regular way until an inch shows.

Step 2: Then, take the stapled sheets and insert the *bottom edge* of the sheet to be corrected *underneath* the blank sheet, and turn the platen backward to the point of correction. Manuscripts of any thickness can be corrected in this manner.

4. How to Reverse a Post Card Without Removing It from the Typewriter

Here is a method that will work like *magic!*

Step 1: Insert the card and address it. Then give the platen (or roller) a quick turn. This action flips the bottom edge of the card back over the platen.

Step 2: Continue turning the platen. The platen engages the bottom edge of the card and the card is automatically reversed and re-inserted without adjustment, ready for typing on the other side.

5. How to Address Envelopes in Quantity

You can address envelopes in quantity 50 percent faster if you follow this easy method:

a. Insert the first envelope in the typewriter in the usual way.

b. Then, insert the second envelope when the first is half-way in.

c. Next, address the first envelope.

d. Then, follow by inserting the third when the second is half-way in.

e. Address the second envelope.

f. Then, follow with the fourth, etc., in a continuous chain.

6. How to Make Notations on the Carbon

Notations which are to appear *only* on the carbon copies are made by inserting a piece of paper (or card) over the original, and typing directly on top of the piece of paper (or card). When the paper (or card) is removed, there will be no impressions left on the original.

7. How to use the tabulator

For fast, easy typing, your tabulator can save you time and nervous energy if you set it for the following:

a. Paragraph indentations
b. Subheads
c. Subindentations
d. Date lines
e. Signatures

Of course, for statistical or columnar typing, tabular settings are *essential*.

8. How to rule horizontal or vertical lines

Ruling lines requires no artistic ingenuity. Here is how you can easily rule pencil or pen lines while the sheet is in the typewriter.

For horizontal lines, place the pencil or pen in the "notch" or "hole" located in the lower corner of the card-holding guide. Then, move the carriage from left to right and rule the required number of spaces.

When drawing vertical lines, disengage the line position reset and roll the platen up and down.

9. How to make erasures at the bottom of the page

When erasures are to be made at the bottom of the page, roll the sheet backward to avoid losing alignment. Then, make the erasure.

10. How to keep from typing too close to the bottom of the page

If fear of typing near the bottom of the page becomes a mental strain, simply make a light pencil mark on the left margin of the paper about 2½ inches from the bottom of the sheet, before inserting it in the typewriter. When you see the pencil mark, you will be readily warned.

Your ability to apply all of the above shortcuts to your daily typing will enable you to do your job *better* and *faster*.

SOME HELPFUL HINTS

1. Change your typewriter ribbon frequently. A *worn* ribbon provides illegible copy.

2. To prevent the keys from cutting through the sheet of paper, place another sheet directly behind it. The extra sheet cushions the blow of the keys as they strike the paper.

3. If too much pressure on the letter "o" cuts a hole through the paper, it can easily be mended by making a tiny *paper patch* of the same quality on the reverse side of the sheet and taping it down with transparent tape, if available. The size of the patch should be a little larger than the size of the letter "o."

Caution: If several holes have appeared on the sheet, do not try to patch all of them. It is best to retype the page. Too many patches tend to create a sloppy appearance.

HOW TO CARE FOR YOUR TYPEWRITER

Like every secretary, you will want a typewriter that is in "top-notch" condition so that it will enable you to produce your work accurately and neatly. You simply cannot make any impression of efficiency on a typewriter that is in poor condition. If it needs adjustment or overhauling, call a serviceman immediately.

To gain full satisfaction from your typewriter and to prolong its life, it is necessary that you treat it well.

Said one secretary, "My typewriter is like a baby. The more care I give it, the better it behaves. I'm able to turn out clean, neat work with less effort."

Here are some DO's for proper care of your typewriter:

Cleaning the Type

1. As often as possible, dust the exterior and accessible parts of your machine with a brush or a lint-free cloth.
2. Lightly dust the type bars toward you.
3. Move the carriage to the extreme right and left and wipe the exposed surfaces of the carriage rails with a dry cloth.
4. Clean the type with a dry bristle brush, with a brushing motion toward you and away from the type basket.
5. If you use a cleaning fluid, moisten the cloth only slightly and dab the type faces lightly.

Removing the Platen

1. Center the carriage, raise tops of paper bail carriage end covers and copy guide.
2. Lift up latches. Then lift out platen.
3. The feed rolls are now accessible for cleaning.

Cleaning Platen, Feed Rolls, and Bail Rolls

1. To assure proper feeding of the paper and to prevent feed-roll or bail markings, clean the platen, feed rolls, and bail rolls periodically.
2. If you type many stencils or mats, frequent cleaning is suggested.

Replacing Platen

1. To replace platen, center the groove in the right platen shaft on the carriage end plate and bring latches forward and down.
2. When replacing deflector, place back edge in first.

A few DON'Ts to observe:

1. Don't erase directly over the printing point. Move the carriage a little to the left or right so that the erasure grit will fall onto the typewriter's dust-protecting shields or the desk or typewriter table.

2. Don't tie your eraser to your typewriter. It can become caught in the working parts of the machine.

3. Don't use a pin to clean the type. A brush is safe and thorough.

4. Don't use oil on your machine. The oil may come in contact with rubber parts and cause damage to your machine.

5. Don't leave the current turned on when your electrical typewriter is not in use. Unnecessary wear on the motor is apt to shorten its life.

Because the exclusive features of your typewriter are designed to give you maximum typing performance, proper care of your typewriter is *very important*. Keeping your typewriter in good working condition is certain to improve your typing skill.

SUMMARY

There are several ways by which you can exhibit your ability and superiority in your job. One way is by having a thorough knowledge and *expert* control of your typewriter. It is the *key* to typing your way upward toward greater responsibilities and future advancement.

In spite of the ever-increasing complexities of modern business, the typewriter is one device that has helped the secretary to make her office life more efficient, more pleasant, and more rewarding.

Chapter 6

BUSINESS LETTER

AND REPORT WRITING

How much should a secretary know about business-letter writing?

Answer: She should know as much as she can about the subject. The extent of a secretary's knowledge of business-letter writing does not end with the correct transcribing of her shorthand notes. It goes further, much further.

Her ability to put the contents of the letter in correct form so that it will give a favorable appearance to her executive's personality and hers is a valuable business asset.

Also, the skill with which she handles the company's correspondence helps to increase sales and profits by promoting good relations with customers and the general public. The more effectively she performs this part of her job, then, the more successful she is.

Because letter writing is one of the most important business functions, you are required to type perfect letters.

What is a perfect letter?

A perfect letter must be accurate. The name of the addressee, the address, the date, and other pertinent data, all must be correct. Grammar, punctuation, and the meaning of each sentence must likewise be correct. Finally, the letter must be mechanically accurate so that it presents a neat appearance.

THE APPEARANCE OF THE LETTER

A neat letter, besides impressing your executive, has *two* advantages.

1. The reader is influenced not only by the contents of the letter, but also by its physical form and appearance.

2. A neat letter which attracts favorable attention has a better chance of success than a carelessly typed letter.

Neatness is of prime importance for the physical make-up of the letter, but other factors are also important. These include the selection of stationery, the quality of typing, and the folding of the letter.

STATIONERY

Many companies use white bond letterhead paper 8½ by 11 inches in size for most of their regular business correspondence. Some business concerns prefer to use smaller sizes, the 7¼ by 10½ inches, or the 5½ by 8½ inches for brief messages that are more informal in nature. Regardless of the size paper that you are required to use, it is important that you take particular care as to the placement of the letter on the sheet of paper.

TYPING

Clean, accurate typing which conveys a neat appearance holds the reader's interest. Noticeable errors and strikeovers are evidence of careless typing, and indicate that little care was taken in the preparation of the letter.

Folding the Letter

How the letter is folded is also important. Your letter will be neat and easy to open if you follow these directions when folding it.

For a small envelope:

1. Bring the lower edge of the letter up to about one-half inch from the top of the sheet and crease.

Example:

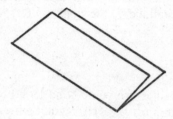

2. Then fold from right to left more than one-third the width of the sheet.

Example:

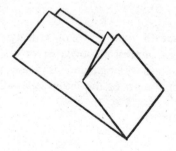

3. Finally, fold from left to right and crease again, leaving at least one-quarter inch uncovered by the left fold.

Example:

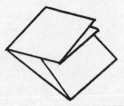

For a long envelope:

1. Fold a little less than a third of the letter from the bottom toward the top of the sheet and crease.

Example:

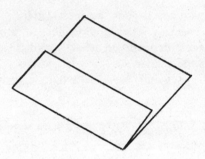

2. Then fold upward to within about one-half inch of the top and crease again.

Example:

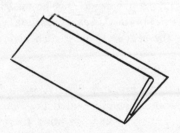

A word of caution: Always make sure the creases are parallel to the edges of the sheet.

FUNCTIONS OF BUSINESS-LETTER WRITING

Almost all of today's business is done completely or partly by mail. Remember, each letter that you write provides an opportunity to make a good impression. It can mean more friends, more customers, and greater profits for your company and your executive.

What is the purpose of a business letter?

A business letter is prepared: (1) to give information; (2) to request information; (3) to influence the reader; (4) to promote sales.

What constitutes a good business letter?

A good business letter is intended to produce the desired results. Its success depends on what is said to induce a favorable response from the reader.

Five basic elements are essential in organizing a successful letter.

1. Definite Purpose. Adequate preparation, clear thinking, and exact expression are necessary for writing effective business letters. The message of your letter should be expressed accurately and concisely. The main ideas should be developed without losing the reader's interest. Too many words take up his time. Too few words may not tell him enough. And little or no attention to sentence structure and proper usage may be misleading.

An important point: Always conclude your letter in such a way as to move the reader to take such action as you desire him to take.

2. Consideration For the Reader. Each letter that you write is intended to produce results which are beneficial to your company; therefore, you must keep in mind the effect that your letter will have on the reader. Three factors have considerable bearing on the reader's final judgment.

a. Use words which the reader can easily understand.

b. Make the tone of your letter reflect your attitude toward the correspondent and toward the subject.

c. Always end your letter in a pleasant manner.

3. Natural Style. The style of modern business letters is usually conversational. It should be remembered that letters involve contacts between two people. Their personalities, as they would emerge in conversation can be transmitted through the mail. Therefore, your letter should indicate your sincerity, warmth, friendship, and efficiency.

4. Correct Usage and Form. An effective letter is one that is free of errors and accurate in every detail. The form of the letter regarding the address, salutation, and complimentary close should also conform to modern business standards.

5. Word Power. No vocabulary is good unless it is *accurate*. The more facility you have with words the easier it will be to express yourself. An important aid to clarity lies in short, simple words and easy-to-read sentences.

A helpful suggestion: To be certain that your letter will attract a favorable response from the reader, every time you write a letter, ask yourself these questions:

a. Does the letter consider the reader?

b. Is the reason for the letter clear? Does it say what I mean it to say?

c. Is the letter unified and coherent?

d. How is the sentence structure?

e. Is it too wordy?

f. Are any words or phrases objectionable? If so, leave them out.

THE ESSENTIAL QUALITIES OF
GOOD CORRESPONDENCE

The message in your letter is not the only factor which influences the reader. He is influenced also by its physical form and appearance. As already mentioned, the reader's first impression depends largely on the care that was taken in the preparation and the typing of the letter. Since such first impression can have considerable bearing on his final judgment, you should check the following physical elements carefully before the letter is mailed.

1. The envelope.
Your letter begins with the envelope. (See Figure 1.)
a. Stationery of good quality should be used.
b. Use first-class mail.
c. Envelopes should be individually typed.
d. The appearance of the envelope should be neat.

2. The format.
a. The letterhead should convey the necessary information about your company.
b. The format of the letter should be pleasing.
c. The letter should be easy to read.
d. The page should not be cluttered with a lot of typing.
In choosing a particular format, you should consider the relative advantages of the various formats for your purposes. Several standard formats in current use offer choices of (a) Block or indented form; (b) Open or closed punctuation; (c) Or, a combination of these. (See Figures 2, 3, and 4.)

3. The necessary parts of any letter consist of:
a. The heading or letterhead
b. Date
c. Inside Address

    d. Salutation
    e. Body
    f. Complimentary Close
    g. Signature
    h. Initials

Other optional parts such as postcripts, notations of enclosures, attention lines, and special references may also be included.

4. Points to observe concerning the particular parts of a letter.

The Date. Avoid eccentricities of form. The following are acceptable:

September 11, 19—   11 September 19—

Note: Avoid abbreviating the name of the month.

Inside Address. The inside address should follow the letterhead of the concern addressed. Remember, *Company* or *Incorporated* should be abbreviated only if it is done in the official name of the corporation.

Title of Person. Always use the correct title of the person addressed. Where possible, include the person's given name or initials.

    a. In other than formal usage, a civil, military, or naval title preceding a name is abbreviated if followed by given name or initial; but *Mr., Mrs., M., MM., Messrs., Mlle., Mme.,* and *Dr.* are abbreviated with or without given name or initial.

    b. *Sr.* and *Jr.* should not be used without given name or initials, but may be used in combination with any title.

    Example: J. B. Jones, Jr.; John B. Jones, Jr., *not* Jones, Jr., *nor* Mr. Jones, Jr.; President J. C. Allen, Jr.

    c. The abbreviation *Esq.,* not generally used in the United States, and other complimentary titles such as *Mr., Mrs.,* and *Dr.*

```
Your Company Name
Street Address
City and State (Zip Code)


            Mr. Edward F. Falkner, President
            ABC Tool Company, Inc.
            1234 Main Street
            Chicago, Illinois (Zip Code)
```

```
Your Company Name
Street Address
City and State (Zip Code)


            ABC Tool Company, Inc.
            1234 Main Street
            Chicago, Illinois (Zip Code)



 Attention: Mr. James H. Donnelly
```

```
Your Company Name
Street Address
City and State (Zip Code)


            Mr. William E. Brown
            c/o Sheraton Hotel
            Chicago, Illinois (Zip Code)



 Hold for Arrival
```

Sample Envelopes
(Figure 1)

(Letterhead) Company Name
Street Address, City, State (Zip Code)
Telephone Number

September 26, 19--

Mr. Edward R. Smith, President
ABC Tool Company
1234 Main Street
Chicago, Illinois (Zip Code)

Dear Mr. Smith:

_____
_____
_____

_____
_____
_____
_____

_____
_____

Sincerely yours,

William E. Brown
Office Manager

WEB/mel

Block Style
(Figure 2)

(Letterhead) Company Name
Street Address, City, State (Zip Code)
Telephone Number

September 26, 19--

Mr. Edward R. Smith, President
ABC Tool Company
1234 Main Street
Chicago, Illinois (Zip Code)

Dear Mr. Smith:

_____

Sincerely yours,

William E. Brown
Office Manager

WEB/mel

Indented Style
(Figure 3)

(Letterhead) Company Name
Street Address, City, State (Zip Code)
Telephone Number

September 26, 19--

Mr. Edward R. Smith, President
ABC Tool Company
1234 Main Street
Chicago, Illinois (Zip Code)

Dear Mr. Smith:

_____
_____
_____

_____
_____
_____
_____

_____
_____

                        Sincerely yours,

                        William E. Brown
                        Office Manager

WEB/mel

Semi-block Style
(Figure 4)

should not appear in combination with any other title or with abbreviations indicating scholastic degrees.

Examples: Henry C. Blake, Esq., *not* Mr. Henry C. Blake, Esq., *nor* Henry C. Blake, Esq., A.M.; *but* John L. Smith, Jr., Esq. George Brown, A.B., Ph.D.; *not* Mr. George Brown, A.B., Ph.D.; Allen Gray, M.D., *not* Mr. Allen Gray, M.D., *nor* Dr. Allen Gray, M.D.

d. The titles *Senator, Representative, Commodore* and *Commandant* are not abbreviated.

e. Unless preceded by *the,* abbreviate *Honorable, Reverend* and *Monsignor* when followed by the first name, the initials or the title.

f. When name of person is followed by abbreviations designating religious and fraternal orders and scholastic and honorary degrees, their sequence is as follows: Orders, religious first; theological degrees, academic degrees earned in course; and honorary degrees in order of bestowal. William G. Brown, D.D., A.M., D.Lit.; E. W. Kramer, C.S.C., St.T. Lr., Ph.D., LL.D.

g. Academic degrees standing alone may be abbreviated. *Examples:*

Henry was graduated with a B.A. degree; *but* bachelor of arts degree (lowercase if spelled out).

He earned his Ph.D. by hard work.

Attention Line. An attention line may come between the inside address and the salutation. Sometimes it is on the same line as the salutation. Usually in such cases, the salutation is *Gentlemen:*

The Salutation. The salutation may be formal, standard, or informal.

Examples:

Formal: Dear Sir:
                          Sir:
                          My dear Sir:

Standard: Dear Mr. Jones:
                          My dear Mr. Jones:

Informal: Dear Bill:
                          Dear Jones:

Complimentary Close. The complimentary close also may be formal, standard, or informal.

Examples:
The formal close:
Very truly yours,   (most frequently used)
Yours very truly,   (sometimes used)

Yours truly,
Truly yours,   (are becoming rare)

The standard close:
Sincerely yours or *Sincerely* is suitable when some friendly contact with the reader has already been established.

The informal close:
Cordially yours or *Cordially* may be used in writing to a personal acquaintance.

Frequently, you see letters close with *Best regards*. There is nothing wrong with that, particularly when you know the person well.

Respectfully yours is occasionally used in writing to an older person, an employer, a government official, or some other person toward whom it is desired to show special consideration.

Note: A comma usually follows the complimentary close. However, some companies using open punctuation prefer to omit it.

The Signature. The signature consists usually of the name of the writer and his business title (if any).

When a secretary signs a letter in the writer's absence, she writes his name in her *own* handwriting and puts her initials below the last few letters of the signature.

Example:

Very truly yours,

William E. Brown
Assistant Treasurer

Examples:

Women should indicate their marital status in the typed name beneath their signatures. A married woman, widow or divorcee does not sign her husband's given name. The following are correct:

Single Woman: Very truly yours,

                          Mary A. Brown

                          Very truly yours,

                          (Miss) Mary A. Brown

Married Woman: Very truly yours,

                           Mary A. Jones
                           (Mrs. John J. Jones)

Divorced Woman: Very truly yours,

                           (Mrs.) Mary Brown Jones

Note: Widows and divorced women retain the title (Mrs.) unless it has been legally changed. It is not correct form if a divorced woman uses her husband's name or initials.

Enclosure. When an enclosure is sent with a letter, a notation to that effect should be put directly below the initials.

Examples:

JB/mel	JB/mel	JB/mel
Enc.	Enclosure	Enclosures: 2

JB/mel	JB/mel
Encl.	2 encls.

Postscripts. Common sense should be used regarding postscripts. A postscript may occasionally be used to emphasize a special point, not merely to call attention to something that the writer inadvertently omitted. The postscript is typed two spaces below the initials.

Examples:

JB/mel   JB/mel

P.S. (Postscript message)   Enc.

                                              P.S. (Postcript message)

Second Sheets. When a letter runs over to the second page, it is usually continued on a blank sheet of bond paper. No letterhead is required. However, some companies prefer to use a second sheet with the name of the company printed along the top edge of the sheet.

At the top of the page, type the name of the recipient, the page number and the date. (See Figures 5 and 6.)

Example 1:
Mr. E. R. Smith   —2—   September 26, 19—

Example 2:
Mr. E. R. Smith
Page 2
September 26, 19—

TYPES OF BUSINESS LETTERS

Every business letter is designed to achieve a particular objective. Every letter that you write conveys a picture of your personality, your service, and your company. That picture can be good or bad, depending on how your letter is written. A good letter should reflect a pleasant, friendly attitude. Remember, it's the tone of your letter that matters. If proper principles are applied to the preparation of each letter, successful results should be obtained.

What kind of business letters do most firms send out?

There are several kinds: (1) Routine Business Letters; (2)

Mr. Edward R. Smith
Page 2
September 26, 19--

_____
_____
_____
_____
_____

_____
_____
_____

_____
_____
_____

Sincerely yours,

William E. Brown
Office Manager

WEB/mel

(Name of Company, if preferred)

-2-
Mr. Edward R. Smith   September 26, 19--

——————————————————————————
——————————————————————————
——————————————————————————
——————————————————————————
————————————

——————————————————————————
——————————————————————————
————————————————————————

——————————————————————————
——————————————————————————
————————————————

                        Sincerely yours,

                        William E. Brown
                        Office Manager

WEB/mel

Continuing Page
Semi-block or Indented Style
(Figure 6)

Courtesy Correspondence; (3) Customer Correspondence; (4) Sales Letters; (5) Letters of Application; (6) Business Reports.

ROUTINE BUSINESS LETTERS

Routine letter writing constitutes a major part of the daily business routine. Routine business letters fall into three general categories: (1) Inquiries and Replies; (2) Announcements, Invitations, and Appointments; (3) Orders, Acknowledgments of Orders, and Remittances.

I. Inquiries and Replies

Business transactions are often the result of an exchange of correspondence involving inquiries and replies. A properly written inquiry can help to bring valuable information that may save dollars or make a profit. An effective reply most likely will build good will and increase sales. Therefore, the clearer and the more complete your inquiry is, the more satisfactory the reader's response is likely to be.

A. INQUIRIES

Besides seeking information, letters of inquiry have two main purposes: (1) Asking favors; and (2) Seeking sales possibilities.

Asking Favors. When a favor is being sought, in the shape of asking for material or information, the following should be observed:

a. Indicate the purpose of your letter and state why you have addressed that particular person.

b. Ask the necessary questions clearly and directly; and, as always, keep your letter brief to save reading time.

c. Indicate the use to which you will put the information or material.

   d. Enclose a stamped, addressed envelope for the reply.

   e. Close the letter with an expression of appreciation for the requested material.

Gentlemen:

    I am presently engaged in research for a magazine article on computer data processing.

    As manufacturer of the world's leading computer system, you may possibly be able to send me some helpful literature about your model X-204.

    I am confident that I will find much of value for my purpose in this material, which I shall be happy to have. Enclosed is a stamped, addressed envelope for your reply.

            Very truly yours,

Seeking Sales Possibility. When writing letters seeking information with regard to a sales possibility, the following elements are essential:

   1. Indicate the product or service that you require.

   2. Request the necessary data and facts that might be useful to you in making a decision. It will be helpful also if you ask for the name of a sales representative, a demonstration, etc.

   3. Close the letter with a courteous request for a prompt reply.

Gentlemen:

    Your firm has been recommended to us as an outstanding manufacturer of office duplicating machines.

    We would like to know your charge for keeping five E-Z Copiers in our offices; also the charges for the various sizes of paper the machines take.

    If you decide to send a sales repre-

sentative, please have him call between ten
and eleven in the morning.

> Very truly yours,

B. REPLIES TO INQUIRIES

Letters in response to inquiries require care and tact. Depending upon the inquiry, your reply may be either affirmative or negative.

Affirmative Response to Inquiries. Courtesy is the main factor in preparing this type of letter. Four elements constitute a good reply.

1. Thank the writer for the letter, and indicate your appreciation for his interest.

2. Supply the requested information and any additional material that might be useful or necessary.

3. If the request is for something other than information, indicate when it will be complied with. If there will be a delay, explain the reason.

4. Close by expressing your willingness to serve further.

Note: If the inquiry is not clear, always request additional information tactfully.

Dear Mr. Harvey:
    Thank you for your letter of March 15.
    Your inquiry about our computer system
greatly interests us.
    We are glad to send you the enclosed
booklet "Basic Facts About The X-204." We
hope this is what you need.
    If we can be of further assistance,
please let us know. We shall be most happy
to see your article when it is in print.

> Very truly yours,

Negative Response to Inquiries. A reply turning down an inquiry is generally rather a difficult letter to write. Here, again, tact is the main factor. To aid you in formulating your refusal, here are three suggestions:

1. Express your regret tactfully.
2. Give adequate reason for your refusal.
3. Be concise and courteous, but firm.

```
Dear Mr. Lawrence:
     Thank you for sending me the outline for
your book HOW TO BE A SUCCESSFUL EXECUTIVE.
     There is no question that it is thor-
oughly competent and will undoubtedly find
an audience to whom it will be valuable.
That audience, however, seems to us rather
specialized for our trade list; too much so
for us to be able to make an offer to take
it on.
     I wish you the best of luck in finding
a house for it. The material is being
returned to you under separate cover.
                         Very truly yours,
```

II. Announcements, Invitations and Appointments

You may have occasion at one time or another to prepare an announcement, send out an invitation, or announce someone's appointment to office. These letters may be either formal or informal. In any case, here again courtesy and conciseness are essential.

1. *Announcement letters* usually tell about a special event, describe a new product, or tell something about a new service, etc. Observe the following:

Dear Mr. Henderson:
     Because of our great respect for the
New York Times, which I am certain you
share, we wanted to be sure that you saw
the enclosed article from last Sunday's
magazine section.
     I believe you will agree that this ob-
jective reporting piece has a lot to tell all
of us about the importance of pretesting and
the task of turning out more effective advertising.
                         Very truly yours,

Note: Formal announcements are frequently made up on
printed cards.

     2. *Letters of invitation* may vary. The writer may wish to
bid for new business. He may want to welcome a new resident
to the community, or to offer good wishes to a new business
establishment. He may want to invite someone to attend a business luncheon or meeting, or to appear as a guest. He might
even want to suggest a way of solving a personal or a business
problem.

Invitation to appear as a guest at a luncheon meeting:

Dear John:
     The time is drawing near when we must
consider additional persons to be nominated
to the Advertising Hall of Fame, which is
co-sponsored by the American Advertising
Federation and the Advertising Club of
New York.
     We would be honored if you would agree
to serve as a member of the judging committee. Through your broad experience in the

advertising profession, I know that you
would be of real service to this committee.
     The luncheon meeting to elect this year's
member(s) to the Hall of Fame is scheduled
for Friday, May 12, at 12:30 p.m. I would
appreciate it greatly if you would accept
this invitation to serve.

                              Sincerely,

3. *Letters of appointment* usually announce the designation or the placing in office of someone who is to fill a vacancy by appointment. There is another type of appointment letter which constitutes an agreement for two or more persons to meet at a designated time and place.

Announcing the designation of someone in office:

Dear Mr. Howard:
     Thomas W. Farrell has been named manager
of the Seattle office of ABC Tool, replacing
Arnold P. Strong who has resigned.
     Tom previously worked as marketing man-
ager for Comstock, Inc., in Seattle for
several years. In this capacity he was re-
sponsible for sales and promotion of the
Heavy-Duty lawn mower.
     We believe Tom's experience in the mar-
keting of various other garden implements
will be beneficial to us in serving all our
customers in the Seattle area.

                        Very truly yours,

Agreement for two persons to meet at a designated place:

Dear John:
     I will be delighted to meet you for

lunch Thursday, October 15, at the University
Club at 12:15 p.m.
It will be a great pleasure to see you
again.

Sincerely yours,

III. *Orders, Acknowledgments of Orders, and Remittances*

A large volume of today's business activities deals with the
preparation of letters that involve orders and payments for merchandise. Most of these letters are sent to the company's customers and suppliers, and proficiency in writing letters about
orders and remittances is certain to increase good will towards
the company.

A. ORDER LETTERS AND REPLIES

Because order letters involve such matters as the description
of merchandise, catalog numbers, amounts of money, terms and
delivery dates, they must be exact in every detail. Replies to them
should be cordial and tactful.

1. Writing Orders. In writing an order letter, it is most important to make it correct and complete so that it can be filled
exactly as you wish. Errors or incompleteness may result in further correspondence, unnecessary adjustments in billing, delays
in shipping, repacking, or even loss of business.

To save undue complications in the filling of orders, many
large mail-order companies provide order forms for their customers. When an order form is provided, a letter is *not* needed. Customers should use the order forms, whenever possible, in pref-
erence to the letters.

If no order form is used, preciseness is the chief quality to
be sought.

a. Give complete and exact information concerning the merchandise ordered.

b. Give specific directions for shipment such as: (1) day and date that shipment is to be made; (2) manner of shipment —parcel post, railway express, air express, etc.

c. Indicate the method of payment.

d. Indicate any special need for promptness.

Note: A follow-up letter should be written if an order is delayed, and has not been acknowledged.

```
Gentlemen:
     Please deliver to the above address the
following items by express, prepaid:
     10 Pints, White Plastic Paint,
          $1.10 a pint ..................$11.00
     10 Quarts, White Enamel Paint,
          $2.15 a quart ................ 21.50
     Please deliver these items no later than
two weeks from the date of this order.
     Enclosed is our check for $32.50.
                         Very truly yours,
```

2. Replying to Order Letters. Ordinarily, an order letter does not need a reply. However, there are circumstances when a reply to an order is necessary or helpful. In such cases, replies to orders may be prepared to: (a) Acknowledge an order; (b) Request additional information; (c) Refuse an order.

Acknowledgments. Acknowledgment of an order is usually made if a delay in filling it is expected. Four essentials constitute a good acknowledgment letter.

a. First, thank the customer for the order.

b. Give information identifying the order.

c. State the reason for the delay and when the order will be filled.

d. Close with an expression of pleasure in serving your customer.

> Dear Mr. Bronson:
> Thank you for your order dated October 15 for ten pints of White Plastic Paint at $1.10 a pint and ten quarts of White Enamel Paint at $2.15 a quart.
> We shall be happy to send you the ten pints of White Plastic Paint. We regret to tell you that due to an unusually heavy demand, our stock of White Enamel Paint is temporarily depleted. However, a new supply is expected in a few days; and we will see that your order of ten quarts of White Enamel Paint is delivered to you immediately.
> We welcome the opportunity to serve you again; and we hope the delay will not inconvenience you.
> > Very truly yours,

Special reasons may also prompt a reply. As a matter of routine, some companies send acknowledgment letters to a new customer to say "thank you" to him and to make him feel that his business is valued. A routine acknowledgment of this sort, by promoting good relations with the customer, may help to increase business.

Requesting Additional Information. If an order is incomplete, your reply should be written tactfully so that you can secure clarification of the essential information that you need. Begin by thanking the customer for his order. *A word of caution:* Instead of emphasizing the customer's error, concentrate on ways to speed up the order to him that will comply with his wishes.

Dear Mrs. Watkins:
        Thank you for your order of April 15
for one dozen towels.
        The particular towel you selected comes
in both the bath size and the regular size.
Before we can fill your order, we shall need
further information regarding the size.
        We shall be ready to ship your order
just as soon as we receive your answer.
                              Very truly yours,

Refusing Orders. When an order has to be refused, in a
direct, tactful, but *firm* manner, you should express regret and
explain briefly why the order cannot be filled. For example:
        1. Perhaps an item is out of stock. You should tell the cus-
tomer when it will be back in stock.
        2. Or, perhaps the item has been discontinued. If possible,
you should suggest an alternate way of obtaining the goods.
        3. To show that you want to be of assistance in every way
possible, you might even offer a substitute.
        Patience in explaining the situation helps to retain the cus-
tomer's good will. *A reminder:* Be sure that you thank the customer for the order.

Dear Mrs. Stewart:
        We are glad to acknowledge your order
of December 15 for the 52-piece service of
bone-china dinnerware in the wheat design.
        We regret to tell you that this par-
ticular pattern has been discontinued. It
has been replaced by a similar pattern shown
on page 4 of the enclosed catalog.
        Should you wish to substitute this pat-
tern for the one you ordered, or should you
decide on something entirely different,
please let us know.
                              Very truly yours,

B. REMITTANCE LETTERS

Almost all types of remittance letters involve matters that deal with money, the correction of errors, or some irregularity in payment.

Remittance letters are usually written for the purpose of: (1) Transmitting payment; (2) Acknowledging payment; (3) Noting errors in billing; (4) Calling attention to payment errors.

What constitutes a good remittance letter?

The two requirements for writing remittance letters are tact and accuracy. People are often sensitive about the payment of bills, so tact is required in regard to the subject. Accuracy is necessary because the letters involve amounts, dates, terms, invoice numbers, etc. Any inaccuracy concerning these items may create ill will. Therefore it is essential that you take particular care regarding the correctness of this type of letter. As a measure of precaution, analyze and review such letters carefully before they are sent. Tact and accuracy are prime assets.

COURTESY CORRESPONDENCE

You can train yourself to write good letters. Once you've acquired the skill, you will find it takes no more effort to write a good letter than it does to write a poor one. The main objective here is to build good will.

When you write a letter, think in terms of *how the other person is likely to react to it*. The tone of your letter is what counts. You must be able to convey any message, even an unpleasant one, in a friendly, courteous way so that it won't hurt the reader's feelings.

Your letters will have less chance of antagonizing the other person if you will remember: It isn't *what you say,* it is *how you say it* that will win his friendly attitude. Tact, therefore, is the main factor in writing courtesy letters. A courtesy letter may be written for the following reasons:

1. Requesting information or material

Suppose you are writing a letter in which you are seeking a favor of some kind, it is best if you:

    a. State the request specifically in a clear-cut manner.
    b. Give the reason for your request.
    c. Close on a courteous note of appreciation.

```
To the Office Manager:
     Your reply to the enclosed questionnaire
will help to determine the sales potential
of my new book HOW TO BE A SUCCESSFUL EX-
ECUTIVE which is currently being considered
for publication by a well-known publisher
of business books.
     I am an executive with the ABC Tool
Company. I also give lectures in executive
training. Most of the material in the book
is now being used in my lectures; and the
response of my audiences has been most
gratifying.
     In order to determine the usefulness of
this new book, the publisher has asked me
to obtain comments on its merit from office
managers of leading business firms. I would
greatly appreciate it if you will kindly
answer the two questions in the enclosed
questionnaire and return it to me in the
enclosed stamped, addressed envelope. I shall
welcome your comments.
     Thank you for your kind interest and
cooperation.
                    Very truly yours,
```

Note: If you are seeking the other person's cooperation, be sure to be specific in indicating the time, place, and nature of the cooperation that is desired.

2. *Granting a request for information or material*

No matter how much or how little information you are able to give, a courteous reply to a request creates a favorable impression. The reader will be grateful for whatever help he receives. In granting a favor, the following suggestions are recommended.

1. Indicate what favorable action is to be taken.

2. Suggest your interest in the work of your correspondent.

3. Make any further comment on what is being done and give any needed explanation.

4. Finally, indicate your willingness to give further assistance.

Granting a request for material:

```
Dear Bill:
     This is in answer to your letter of
March 15.
     I am glad to send you the list of names
and addresses of the various mail order ad-
vertisers located in the New York area.
     If I can be of any further help to you as
your project develops, don't hesitate to
let me know.
                         Sincerely yours,
```

3. *Declining a request for information or material*

A letter declining a favor is somewhat more difficult to write. Each situation presents an individual problem. However, proper handling of the matter will help to insure good will. In your reply:

a. Give a direct refusal with suitable explanations, and use a courteous tone.

b. Indicate your regret at the need to refuse.

c. If appropriate, express your interest in the work being done.

d. Close the letter courteously and tactfully, suggesting your willingness to give future help, if this seems appropriate.

Declining a request for material:

> Dear Miss Burke:
>   An overwhelmingly heavy demand for the
> booklet "18 Ways To Avoid Office Fatigue"
> prevents us from sending you the six copies
> you requested.
>   There is a possibility that reprints of
> this booklet will be available next month.
> I have made a record of your request, and
> shall see that your copies are sent to you
> immediately.
>   Thank you for your interest in this pub-
> lication. If we can be of further service
> to you in any other way, please let us know.
>   Very truly yours,

4. *Expressing appreciation, congratulations, and praise*

Perhaps you wish to acknowledge your appreciation of a special favor which has been granted. Perhaps you desire to praise someone for consistently good work. Perhaps you want to make note of any outstanding achievement, such as a promotion to a new post, or the like. In any case, letters expressing your appreciation or praise should generally be brief and sincere.

Expressing appreciation:

> Dear Mrs. Patterson:
>   I am ever so grateful to you for taking
> a few minutes from your busy schedule to
> assist me with my project.
>   Thank you for your interest and
> cooperation.
>   Very truly yours,

> Dear Mr. Jones:
>   Thank you very much for your prompt and

very generous response to my solicitation
on behalf of the Hartford Heart Fund.
    Your thoughtfulness not only will help
make the drive itself a success, but also
will contribute to the continued excellence
of this social service in our community.
                Very truly yours,

Expressing congratulations:

Dear Kenneth:
    You can't imagine how delighted I was
to read about your new appointment as senior
vice president. It couldn't have happened
to a nicer person.
    Congratulations and best wishes.
                Sincerely,

5. *Introducing and recommending*

A general letter of recommendation is, naturally, less specific in nature than a specific one. If the recommendation is requested by the person seeking a position, but is not directed to any particular individual, it may be addressed *To Whom It May Concern:*

However, if your letter of recommendation is the *result of an inquiry,* it should be specific. Observe the following:

1. Be candid and precise in your evaluation of the person.
2. Indicate his value as a worker and his contribution to the organization.
3. Indicate the extent of his experience and his potential.
4. Accentuate the positive side of the person, but don't overdo the praise.
5. If appropriate, comment on his personal traits.

Letter of recommendation as the result of an inquiry:

Dear Mr. Bennett:
    In your letter of April 28 you mention

that my name was given to you as reference
by Mr. Edward Johnson.
    Mr. Johnson has been my neighbor for
more than twenty-five years. During that time
I have found him to be an ideal friend—
honest, respectful, conscientious, and willing to be of assistance at all times. In
view of these attributes, I am confident that
he will be a desirable employee of The
Gardner Tool Company.
                        Very truly yours,

Letter to a person named as reference:

Dear Mr. Robertson:
    We have recently employed Edward Johnson
of 200 Oakwood Drive, North Bergen, N.J., who
has given us your name as reference.
    It will help us if you will tell us what
you can of his character and desirability as
an employee.
    Thank you for your reply. A stamped,
addressed envelope is enclosed for your
convenience in replying.
                        Very truly yours,
                        R. W. Bennett

    6. *Acknowledgment by secretary in the writer's absence*
    The following letters suggest an appropriate approach to a
situation, and provide the format of a suitable letter:

Dear Mr. Adams:
    Your letter of April 15 arrived in this
morning's mail. It will be brought to Mr.
Brown's attention when he returns from his
trip to St. Louis. He is expected back within
two weeks.

If you consider the matter urgent enough,
I can give you his hotel address and telephone number in St. Louis.

                    Very truly yours,

Dear Mr. Graham:
    In Mr. Brown's absence I am acknowledging
receipt of your letter of March 15. I will
bring it to his attention when he returns
early next week.

                    Very truly yours,

Dear Mr. Jackson:
    Your letter of June 8 finds Mr. Brown
on vacation. It is being held for his attention when he returns on Monday, June 15.

                    Very truly yours,

Dear Mr. Grant:
    Thank you for your letter of June 30 to
Mr. Brown.
    Mr. Brown is away from the office on
vacation for two weeks and will return
on July 15.
    I have given your letter to Mr. Ander-
son, assistant manager, who, I believe, will
be able to give you the information that
you need.

                    Very truly yours,

Dear Mr. Campbell:
    Thank you for sending along with your
letter of June 1 the transcript of Mr. Gordon's remarks on advertising. Mr. Brown is
away from the office at present, and since
he will not be back for several weeks, I am
passing this correspondence along to Mr.

Stewart, assistant manager, who, I believe,
will enjoy reading Mr. Gordon's discussion.
Upon his return, Mr. Brown will see this
correspondence and I know he will appreciate
your having sent the material to him.
Very truly yours,

Customer Correspondence

Since a great deal of today's business is transacted in writing
letters to customers, your proficiency in writing this kind of letter
effectively contributes substantially to your achieving self-confidence—a necessary quality for business success.

As an effective business-letter writer, you can use your skill
to help increase your company's sales and profits by promoting
good relations with customers. The right approach to an angry
customer can succeed in retaining his business.

Three types of customer correspondence are: (1) Adjustment
Letters, (2) Credit Letters, (3) Collection Letters.

Adjustment Letters

Adjustment letters are prepared to settle complaints with
regard to disputed accounts or claims.

Because handling complaints requires considerable correspondence, many large companies have a special Adjustment and
Complaint Department. Its main function is to investigate and
analyze each complaint. A decision can then be made as to: (1)
whether or not the complaint is justified; and (2) whether or not
the adjustment can be granted.

If the complaint is justified, it is usually the result of: (1)
a fault in the merchandise such as defective, damaged, or incorrect goods; or (2) a fault in service such as delay in delivery,
failure to deliver, or discourtesy on the part of the employees.

If the adjustment is granted, it involves: (1) refunding
money; (2) giving new merchandise; (3) performing an additional service; or (4) simply acknowledging the error and assur-

ing the customer that care will be taken to avoid any repetition.

In dealing with complaints, it is necessary that you first ascertain all the pertinent facts. For this purpose check the files and records.

To be certain that you do a satisfactory job in writing adjustment letters, you should follow certain basic principles:

1. Answer all complaints *promptly*. Making the customer wait only intensifies his dissatisfaction and/or anger.

2. Thank the customer and let him know of your interest. If you can satisfy him, say so at the outset.

3. Tell him tactfully what you can and cannot do for him.

4. Give the customer the benefit of the doubt. Remember, he is right unless the facts prove him wrong.

5. Accept any blame gracefully. If the customer is wrong, tactfully explain why.

6. If the complaint is refused, explain the reason and emphasize any positive aspects of the situation.

7. Be diplomatic. Close the letter in a way that will retain the customer's good will.

A few Don'ts to observe:
Don't betray your anger or impatience.
Don't sound grudging.
Don't be over-apologetic.

CREDIT LETTERS

In business, *credit* is the confidence placed in a purchaser's ability and intention to pay, shown by entrusting him with goods or services, without immediate payment.

Today, many large corporations conduct most of their business on the basis of credit. Credit is instrumental in enabling the producer, the manufacturer, the retailer, and the consumer to obtain goods or services at the time they are needed even when ready cash is not available.

Although in any credit transaction the promise to pay is

important, the customer's intention and ability to meet payments when they are due is even more important.

Credit is granted to a customer on the basis of the following:

1. *Capital*—his net financial worth.

2. *Capacity*—his ability to pay debts when due.

3. *Character*—his reputation, especially with respect to the manner in which he pays his debts.

Information concerning a company's capital, capacity, and character may be obtained from various sources. It is often more difficult to obtain credit information for individuals.

In obtaining credit data for a business concern, inquiries may be directed to:

1. Credit agencies, such as Dun & Bradstreet, Inc.

2. Trade associations, of which the company is a member.

3. The company itself, which may be asked to supply a financial statement, or bank, or trade references.

When obtaining credit information for an individual, the following sources prove helpful:

1. Commercial banks will provide information for individuals who maintain a regular checking account or those who transact business with these banks.

2. In large cities, local retail credit bureaus (cooperative agencies run by merchants) will furnish information concerning an individual's credit rating.

3. Facts regarding a person's character and ability to pay may also be obtained from his employer or his company.

TYPES OF CREDIT LETTERS

Assuming that you are employed in the Credit Department of a large corporation, your daily correspondence will fall into seven categories:

1. Letters Requesting Information. In an effort to secure credit information, your letter should be friendly, tactful, and sincere.

2. *Letters Giving Information.* You may be called upon to furnish information about your own company. Or, you may be asked to furnish information about a firm with which your company does business. In either case, your reply must be courteous and as complete as possible. By demonstrating your understanding of the correspondent's need for credit information and your willingness to cooperate, you are likely to establish a relationship that will influence him favorably toward you and your company in future transactions.

3. *Credit good-will letters.* In such letters, prompt customers are commended and thanked for their early payment.

4. *Letters Granting Credit.* Such letters are ordinarily addressed to new customers. Your message granting credit to a new customer offers another good opportunity to create a favorable impression. It can express your pleasure in opening the account and your anticipation of a pleasant relationship.

5. *Letters Refusing Credit.* Informing the customer of your decision to decline his credit is a crucial matter. This is so because you must make every effort to retain the customer's good will despite your refusal to grant him credit. In such a case, the following suggestions should help you to convey the bad news:

a. Discuss the matter frankly and politely.

b. Since you value the order, try to save it.

c. Sell the customer on your terms. Try to obtain the order on a cash basis.

d. Reveal a thorough understanding of the customer's problem.

e. Tell the customer why his order must be refused. Explain the reports you have received regarding his credit. It is best to consider that they may be wrong.

6. *Letters Inviting New Credit Accounts.* In addition to responding to requests for credit, your job in the Credit Department requires you to search for opportunities to acquire new accounts.

It is generally known that individuals with credit accounts tend to buy more frequently than a person who is a cash customer. A new credit account can be obtained through a well-written letter in which you invite the customer to avail himself of the company's easy credit terms. Your prospects are to be found among present cash customers, or among persons who, you know, are not your regular customers.

7. Letters Reactivating Old Accounts. When a customer with a reputable credit standing stops using his account, it requires skill on your part to get him to resume activity. You may ask him in a letter if your company was in any way at fault. Or, you may attempt to stimulate activity on the account by stressing a positive reason why he should keep his account active. For example: You might remind the customer of a new collection of spring or fall fashions. You might remind him of a "private sale" for charge account customers only. Or, you might offer special shopping conveniences. Perhaps the customer has mislaid his Account Card, so you might suggest an easy way for him to obtain a new one.

Collection Letters

Collection letters are the most difficult letters to write, especially if the customer has not paid at all.

If you are in charge of collecting past-due accounts, familiarize yourself with the necessary factors that make collection letters successful. They are:

1. Knowledge of Your Customers. In addition to having a broad knowledge of human nature, you have to know the specific business background and paying habits of your credit customers. As a writer of collection letters, you should bear in mind that people are generally sensitive about their credit standing. In order to retain their good will and friendship they have to be treated with utmost care.

2. *Systematic Follow-Up.* Systematic follow-up letters become necessary when payments are past due. Through such a system, you remind the customers that you expect prompt payment. The timing of your follow-up letters is an important factor in the success of your collection efforts. Because of differences in paying habits, credit customers fall into three classifications: (1) Very good risks; (2) Good risks; (3) Poor risks.

It requires knowledge and insight to distinguish between the classes of risks and to make proper use of this knowledge. The better the risk, the longer the time you can allow between follow-up letters. A good risk may be sent a letter once a month, while a poor risk, may have to be sent a letter every two weeks. If you utilize an effective follow-up system, you will have fewer overdue accounts and fewer letters to write.

3. *Good Tone.* The most important thing to keep in mind when writing a collection letter is its good tone. Tactful language that will not cause resentment or indifference is most essential, if you want to retain the customer's good will and have him continue to do business with your company.

TYPES OF COLLECTION LETTERS

Among the types of collection letters, there are:

1. Those letters requesting additional payment when not enough money has been enclosed with the order.

2. A similar type are those requesting additional money when payment is made after the normal discount period has elapsed.

3. Collection sales letters. Those in which a customer's delinquent account prevents further orders from being accepted.

Note: Each of the above situations requires individual handling. Remember: Your chief concern is to retain the good will of the customer.

Delinquent accounts are handled in the following manner. A series of letters is written in which five appeals are used in order to obtain payment. (1) Reminders; (2) Inquiries; (3) Appeals to Fairness; (4) Appeals to Self-interest; and (5) Appeals to Fear (or Threats).

Reminders. Reminder letters often do nothing more than casually let the customer know that his account is delinquent. Sometimes they are appeals to *good will* because they take for granted the customer's good intentions. Your first reminder to the customer that his bill is unpaid and that you would like to have payment may say in effect:

> Undoubtedly our account has been overlooked. . . .
> The courtesy of your prompt attention will be greatly appreciated.

Inquiries. Such letters are generally called the discussion stage of the series, in which a motivation is suggested for the customer to pay. If you believe there may be a valid reason why the customer has not cleared his account, you then write a letter to obtain an explanation. The letter merely asks "What is wrong?" and may say, in effect:

> Until now, we have received no response from you regarding the unpaid balance on your account.
> Perhaps there is some reason why payment has not been made. If you are not completely satisfied with your purchase, won't you please write and let us know. We shall be glad to give the matter special consideration.
> If nonpayment is due to an oversight, we hope that you will find it convenient to send us your check within the next few days.

Appeals to Fairness. When the customer fails to acknowledge the first two follow-up messages, your next letter should contain an appeal to fairness. The message may say in effect:

We are very sorry that we must again remind you that your account balance is still past due.

When we opened your account, it was our understanding that we would have the pleasure to serve you to the best of our ability, and that you, in turn, would pay your bills in accordance with our regular credit terms. We have fulfilled our part of the agreement. It is only fair, we believe, that you should fulfill yours.

May we please have your check in full payment by return mail. Thank you for your cooperation.

Your message could stress the point that it is unfair for one customer to have extended time for paying his bills, while other customers are required to pay promptly.

A word of caution: In appealing to fairness, the situation must be handled diplomatically, because people naturally desire to be fair, and any implication to the contrary may create resentment.

Appeals to Self-interest. When circumstances warrant, a letter directed to the customer's self-interest is effective in getting him to make payment. Your message may say, in effect:

We have afforded you every opportunity to pay your long overdue account, but you have neglected to avail yourself of this chance.

As members of the Retail Credit Association, we are bound to turn your delinquent account over to this organization for clearance.

Immediate attention on your part will enable us to withhold reporting your account to the association.

Appeals to Fear. When all other methods to make collection fail, your last resort is the *appeal to fear*. This is the strongest of the collection appeals, because people tend to act when they are threatened by an impending punishment. In appealing to fear, you let the customer know your intent to place his delinquent account in the hands of the company's attorneys *or a collection agency* if payment is not made immediately or within a specified time. Your appeal may say, in effect:

> It is our policy to be fair with our customers. Unfortunately you have not given us this opportunity.
>
> We have made several unsuccessful attempts to help you keep your credit clear, but we were not given your cooperation.
>
> Your account is now so delinquent, that unless payment is made immediately, we shall be forced to place it in the hands of the Retail Credit Association for clearance.

In summary, when writing a series of Collection Letters, there is a time element involved:

1. Early in the series a second letter is sent after a period of 30 days.
2. Then, after a period of two weeks.
3. And still later, after one week.

Sales Letters

A sales letter is a convenient and effective way of securing business. Direct contact and specific appeal are the big advantages of this type of advertising. Sales letters go to large numbers of people, so they should bring valuable returns in dollars and cents.

What is the sales letter designed to do?

An effective sales letter should: (1) attract the attention of the reader; (2) create a desire to purchase the product; (3) convince the reader of the value of the product; and (4) move the reader to take a particular action.

What are the uses of a sales letter?

The sales letter has five principal uses: (1) to sell by mail; (2) to produce sales inquiries; (3) to follow up sales inquiries; (4) to induce people to visit the store to buy; and (5) to build good will.

Because sales letters are highly specialized, it requires exceptional ability and experience to plan a successful sales letter.

1. Analyze your product and emphasize its special advantages.

2. Study the market. Make sure you know the requirements of the particular person or group of persons to whom the letter is to be directed.

3. Know the specific aim of the letter. Is it to bring the customer to the store, or to have him order by mail?

4. Know the special interests of your customer. What is it that would most likely appeal to him. Will you have to awaken a new interest or merely direct his interest to your product?

5. Determine a central selling point—whether it is price or a special quality of goods, and emphasize that.

6. List facts that will support your central selling point.

7. Settle upon a detailed plan of presenting the facts.

Similar to the sales letter is the letter of application, *only* here the product involved is YOU.

Letters of Application

In order to write a successful letter of application, you must, when you are applying for a position, be able to present effectively the *facts* about your character, your ability, and your experience.

Although there are other ways of seeking employment, the method of writing a letter has advantages, for the applicant and for the employer.

1. *For the Applicant*

a. The applicant's letter of application is likely to be a deciding factor in securing an interview, provided his qualifications for a particular job are satisfactory.

b. In securing an interview, the applicant hopes that by means of a personal contact with the personnel manager or department head he will obtain the position he wants.

2. *For the Employer*

a. The letter of application enables the employer to determine the value to his firm of an interview with the applicant.

b. It provides the employer with a permanent record to which he may refer as often as necessary.

Letters of application come under two categories: (1) solicited; and (2) unsolicited.

1. *Solicited Letters.* A solicited letter of application is written in response to an advertisement from the employer. The advantage of writing a solicited letter of application is the certainty that a position is available which the employer is taking steps to fill.

However, the fact that your letter of application is one of many written in response to the same advertisement, indicates that if it is to be accepted, it must be one of the best received.

2. *Unsolicited Letter.* An unsolicited letter of application is written to an employer who has *not* advertised a job opening.

A primary advantage of writing an unsolicited letter is that you *do not* have to compete with other applicants. Also, you can send the same letter to several prospective employers at the same time.

The disadvantages are these: (1) There is a possibility that no job is available. (2) You must be able to determine for yourself the qualifications in which the employer will be most interested.

A successful letter of application has *four* specific functions:

1. *Establishing Favorable Attention.* Since your letter of

application faces considerable competition, it must be businesslike in appearance. It should be neatly written or typewritten on good quality bond paper, 8½ by 11 inches in size. You should write enough to fill at least three-quarters of the page. A short letter may give the impression that you are inadequately qualified.

If your letter of application is to attract favorable attention, you must give particular thought to the phrasing of the opening sentence. The best way to start a *solicited* letter is to state one of your important qualifications for the job. Be sure that this qualification is related to a qualification mentioned in the advertisement.

When you are writing an *unsolicited letter* you do not have a description of the job before you; therefore, you cannot adjust your reply accordingly. The best way to begin an unsolicited letter of application is to name the position that you want. Be as specific as possible. The more specific you are, the more you clarify your goal in the employer's mind.

2. Creating Desire. Your letter of application should create *desire* in the employer's mind for your services and your ability. An orderly plan of presentation and a description of your qualifications accomplishes this objective.

To insure an *orderly presentation of your qualifications,* you should outline them briefly for yourself before you write your letter. Such an outline may include:

a. Age
b. Education
c. Experience
d. Special Qualifications

Suppose you have recently completed high school or college, and as yet have no business experience to write about. In such a case, you may discuss at some length the training you received in school. On the other hand, if you are a person with considerable business background, you can emphasize your experience by giving it top place in your outline.

Also, by describing your qualifications from the employer's point of view, you increase his desire to meet you. This can be achieved if you emphasize the manner in which your qualifications meet the requirements in the employer's advertisement.

To elicit greater interest from the employer, you may state your reasons for desiring to work in the particular field or industry. An employer naturally prefers workers whose interests will make them more enthusiastic about their jobs.

3. Convincing the Employer. You will strengthen your chance of being selected if you back up your appraisal of your qualifications with evidence to support it. Such evidence may consist of: (a) special details; (b) letters of recommendation; (c) names of references; (d) samples of your work; and (e) results of aptitude tests.

4. Stimulating Action. The ultimate aim of your letter of application, of course, is to secure the position. However, few jobs are obtained without a preliminary interview between the employer and the applicant. Therefore, you should close your letter with a courteous request for such an interview. This request will most likely stimulate action on the employer's part. So that you may be easily reached, include your telephone number, if you have one. If you are available for interviews only at certain times, you should say so.

A final thought regarding letters of application: Remember, here as elsewhere, the *tone* of your letter is a determining factor in attracting favorable attention. Besides arousing desire for your services, it provides the prospective employer with a clue to your personality and character. Since the employer is usually concerned about these qualifications, you should take special care in expressing your attitudes. To sound either timid and apologetic or boastful and overconfident makes an unfavorable impression. Instead, a straightforward description of your qualifications is much more effective, especially when it is stated so that the employer is given an opportunity to draw his own conclusions.

If your qualifications meet the requirements for the particular job which is available, you stand a chance of being called for an interview.

BUSINESS REPORTS

Like the letter of application, a business report is an orderly presentation of facts, in this instance involving a specific business activity or program.

A business report is the communicating of information on a particular topic to those persons who can use such information.

Since the basis of the report is fact, it is important that you distinguish between *opinion* and *fact*. If any opinions are to be expressed in your report, they should be solidly based on the facts that are primarily included in the report.

Question: Why write a written report when it is easier to present an oral report?

Answer: Although an oral report does save considerable time, the written report has several advantages:

1. It is more formal and puts more pressure on the writer to be *complete* and *accurate*.
2. The ideas contained in the written report are less likely to be distorted as they are transmitted *directly* from one person to another.
3. It can be retained as a permanent record.
4. It can be referred to as often as necessary.

Among the various classifications of business reports, there are the following:

1. Routine Reports
2. Annual Reports
3. Statistical Reports
4. Sales Reports
5. Progress Reports
6. Operational Reports
7. Record Reports
8. Inspection Reports
9. Period Reports
10. Special Reports

Business reports fall into many classifications. They are most importantly grouped (1) according to purpose—whether informational or analytical and (2) according to format and style.

Several elements must first be considered before you write a report.

1. Type of report—whether it is formal or informal.
2. Purpose of the report.
3. Person or persons toward whom the report is directed.
4. Date the report is due.

How do you obtain facts for your report?

Once you have the idea of the kind of report you are going to write, you begin the actual work of research and composition. This entails: (1) investigating sources of information; (2) taking notes; (3) analyzing the data; (4) making an outline; (5) writing the report.

Investigating Sources of Information. In the course of investigating the sources, it will be helpful if you obtain the facts through: research in libraries; surveys and questionnaires; company files; and personal observation and experience.

Note-Taking. As you are conducting your research, take down notes that will be useful to you in drafting the report. Your notes should be neat and legible. Untidy notes on odd pieces of paper are likely to waste your time in assembling the information. It is more effective to write your notes on white cards, 3 by 5 inches in size. You can then easily arrange your notes according to the specific subjects you want to discuss.

Analyzing the Data. After taking notes, it is a good idea to allow a period of time to analyze all the information you have gathered for your finished report. Careful attention to the *purpose* of the report is essential if the report is to be of value.

1. Analyze the facts; and remember, any conclusion you may wish to state has to be based on *facts*.

2. Include *only* information that will be useful to the reader.

3. Be precise and accurate in your statements. Do not exaggerate.

4. Indicate the degree of reliability of the sources of information you have provided in your report.

5. Maintain careful objectivity and avoid letting your opinions enter into the report.

Caution: In report writing, remember you are presenting *facts,* not *your* opinions. If your report is a good one, it will clearly indicate which portions are facts and which portions are conclusions drawn from facts.

Making an Outline. Once a general idea of the report has taken shape in your mind, a written outline is the most effective way of organizing the mass of details. You will find it easier to draft your report if you follow these basic principles in making the outline:

1. Use headlines and subheads.

2. Construct subheads logically.

3. Make your subheads specific.

4. Number consistently.

5. Utilize your material so that it conforms to the essential points in your outline.

Writing the Report. The final step in preparing your report is actually writing it.

The following procedure will give you an opportunity to test the completeness of the information and to question its validity and accuracy.

1. Use your outline as a guide and follow its order as you write your report.

2. Refer to your notes for the necessary details to fill in the outline.

If your report is to be of value, it should have these qualities: accuracy; clearness; conciseness; careful selection of words; convenience for the reader to use.

The more organized your thoughts are, the better chance you have of getting your message understood.

CHECK LIST FOR EFFECTIVE
LETTER AND REPORT WRITING

The following check list, in question and answer form, should serve as a guide to stimulate more effective letter and report writing.

1. Can anyone write a good letter?

Yes, anyone can write a good letter, if he remembers that each letter he writes is an opportunity to be helpful to some business prospect, customer or supplier, as well as to his own company.

2. How long should your letter be?

It can be as long and only as long as it takes to tell the story *effectively*. A letter designed to *sell* is usually long. A letter designed to *get inquiries* can be shorter—just long enough to get the reader sufficiently interested to ask for more information. A *letter in answer to an inquiry* should be as long as needed to give complete and helpful information. *Collection letters* should be short. If a letter is to *adjust a complaint,* it should be as long as necessary to adjust it satisfactorily.

3. What tools do you need to write good letters?

First, you must have a good command of the English language. Secondly, you must have a desire to make every letter sound friendly.

4. What is the most important quality in a letter?

Tone is the most important quality if you want your letters to make friends. The tone of your letters should reflect your attitude toward the correspondent and toward the subject of the letter. It should also express your sincerity, warmth, and personality. Be sympathetic to your reader's problems and probable reactions. Always end your letters in a pleasant manner.

5. *What are the six essential elements of letter and report writing?*

Each letter that you write should be: (1) clear; (2) correct; (3) complete; (4) concise; (5) convincing; and (6) cordial.

6. *What kind of letter makes the best impression?*

The most effective letter is the one that gets across the idea that you are interested, friendly and eager to be helpful.

7. *What are some good ways to start a letter?*

"Thank you for your letter" or "We are sorry that we are unable to furnish the information requested in your letter of April 10" *express pleasure or regret.* "The table you ordered in your letter of June 2 was shipped by express from our factory today" *shows that action has been taken.* All three are good ways to start a letter.

8. *What are the requirements of a sales letter?*

A sales letter is designed to: (a) arouse the reader's interest; (b) create a desire to buy the product; (c) convince the reader of the value of the product; (d) lead him to take a particular action by making the action easy.

9. *What is the best way to handle a letter of complaint?*

The easiest way to handle a complaint is to put yourself in the customer's place. *Think what the customer is thinking.* Show that you understand his problem, and indicate an attitude that you want to be fair.

10. *What are the rules for writing reports?*

The important thing to remember in writing reports is that you are presenting *facts* not opinions.

a. Organize your thoughts before starting to write.

b. Present them in order of their importance.

c. Indicate the purpose of the report.

d. Give conclusions drawn from the data you have presented.

e. Make your report easy to read and understood.

SUMMARY

The objective in all letter writing is to create a good substitute for a personally delivered message. The more natural your message sounds, the better chance it has of creating the impression you wish to create.

Efficient communication whether by letter or report represents one of today's most important opportunities to save valuable executive time . . . and thus to increase company profits.

Chapter 7

POINTS ON GRAMMAR,

SENTENCE STRUCTURE,

PUNCTUATION

CAPITALIZATION, NUMERALS, AND SPELLING

The purpose of language is *communication*. Good English helps you to communicate your thoughts in writing and speaking. In both your business and social life, you are judged not only on your appearance and your manners, but also on your language. The way you express yourself reflects your breeding, education, and your background. Errors in spelling, pronunciation, or grammatical usage indicate a lack of proper training.

To gain confidence in your command of good English, it is suggested that you acquaint yourself with its fundamental elements.

GRAMMAR

Grammar may be defined as that element of language which deals with classes of words, their relation to each other, and

175

their function in phrases, clauses, and sentences. To most people, grammar is simply speech or writing which conforms to standard usage.

A general understanding of grammar and sentence structure depends on your knowledge of grammatical terms.[1] That is, you must know how to use the various parts of speech, in order to speak and to write correctly.

In any language, words are arranged in classes (called parts of speech) and each class has a name. In the English language, there are eight parts of speech: *noun, pronoun, adjective, verb, adverb, preposition, conjunction* and *interjection.*

THE SENTENCE

A sentence is a group of words so connected as to express one complete thought.

ELEMENTS OF A SENTENCE

A sentence is composed of two essential parts: the subject and the predicate.

The subject in the sentence is a word or group of words about which something is said.

The predicate is that part of the sentence (a word or group of words) which says something about the subject.

EXAMPLES:

We won the race. (Expresses action)
/   /
(Subject) (Predicate)

1. For a more thorough understanding of grammar and sentence structure, see Curme, George O.: *English Grammar,* College Outline Series (New York: Barnes & Noble, Inc., 1947).

The pencil is broken. (Expresses state of being)
/   /
(Subject) (Predicate)

CLASSIFICATION OF SENTENCES

Sentences are classified into two principal groups according to (1) purpose and manner of expression; (2) structure.

A. When classified according to purpose and manner of expression, sentences are divided into four classes: declarative, imperative, interrogative, and exclamatory.

1. Declarative. A declarative sentence merely makes a statement.

EXAMPLE

Today is a holiday.

2. Imperative. An imperative sentence states a command or makes a request.

EXAMPLES:

Do your homework. (Command)
Please do your homework. (Request)

3. Interrogative. An interrogative sentence asks a question.

EXAMPLE:

What is your name?

4. Exclamatory. An exclamatory sentence expresses strong feeling.

EXAMPLES:

I am so sorry!
It is a shame!
What will people think!

B. When classified according to structure, sentences are divided grammatically into four groups, depending on the number and type of clauses they contain: simple, compound, complex, compound-complex.

1. The Simple Sentence. A simple sentence consists of one independent or main clause (a group of words containing a subject and a predicate).

EXAMPLE:

Jane is wearing a red dress.
  /   /
(Subject)   (Predicate)

2. The Compound Sentence. A compound sentence is composed of two or more independent (main) clauses, thus making two complete statements.

EXAMPLE:

The highway is completed, and now it is open to the public.
         /   /
   (Main Clause)   (Main Clause)

3. The Complex Sentence. A complex sentence contains one main (independent) clause and one or more subordinate (dependent) clauses.

EXAMPLE:

Tired and exhausted, after climbing for days,
        /   /
(Subordinate Clause)   (Subordinate Clause)

the climbers reached the top of the mountain.
                    /
            (Main Clause)

4. The Compound-Complex Sentence. A compound-complex sentence is composed of two or more independent (main) clauses and one or more dependent (subordinate) clauses.

EXAMPLE:

After the book was completed, it was published
            /   /
(Subordinate Clause)   (Main Clause)

and it became a great success.
            /
    (Main Clause)

PHRASES

Definition. A phrase is a group of words used as a single part of speech and not containing a subject and a predicate.

KINDS OF PHRASES

Phrases are usually classified as to use and form:

A. Kinds as to Use:

1. A Noun Phrase is a phrase used as a noun.

EXAMPLE:

The speaker of the house called the meeting to order.

2. An Adjective Phrase is a phrase used as an adjective.

EXAMPLE:

The man *in the gray suit* called the meeting to order.

3. An Adverbial Phrase is a phrase used as an adverb.

EXAMPLE:

He spoke *in a loud voice*.

Note: An adverbial phrase usually begins with a preposition.

4. A Verb Phrase is a phrase used as a verb.

EXAMPLE:

He *has gone home*.

B. Kinds as to Form:

Phrases take their names from the kind of word with which they begin, hence the following phrases:

A prepositional phrase consists of a preposition and its object, with or without a modifier.

EXAMPLES:

Mary lives *in town.* (Without a modifier)
Mary lives *in a very small town.* (With a modifier)

A participial, gerund and infinitive phrase consists of a non-finite verb-form with its object or modifier.

EXAMPLES:

The person *cancelling reservations* is very pleasant.
/
(Participial Phrase)

We regretted *cancelling our reservation.*
/
(Gerund Phrase)

We have a good reason *to cancel our reservation.*
/
(Infinitive Phrase)

CLAUSES

Definition. A clause is a group of words that contains a subject and a predicate and is used as a part of a sentence.

Clauses may be classified into (1) Main or Independent Clauses and (2) Subordinate or Dependent Clauses.

Main (Independent) Clause. A main or independent clause is a clause that expresses a complete thought and can stand alone as a sentence.

EXAMPLES:

The clock will run after you wind it.
/
(Main or Independent Clause)

They walked out when I came in.
/
(Main or Independent Clause)

When two or more main or independent clauses are joined into a single (compound) sentence they are called co-ordinate clauses.

Co-ordinate clauses are connected by co-ordinate conjunctions, as *and, also, both, but, either, neither, nor, or, then.*

EXAMPLE:

The sun is shining and _a rainbow is in the sky_, but _it is raining_.

Subordinate (Dependent) Clauses: A subordinate or dependent clause is a clause that does not express a complete thought and cannot stand alone as a sentence.

EXAMPLES:

When he spoke they all listened.

(Subordinate Clause)

After the cast was removed he walked better.

(Subordinate Clause)

Subordinate clauses may be classified according to their grammatical function as noun, adjective, or adverbial clauses.

A Noun Clause is a clause which is used as a noun and is introduced by such words as *that, what, where, when, how, whether,* or *why.*

Functioning as a noun, a noun clause may be used as the object of the verb, the subject, or the predicate nominative.

EXAMPLES:

Object of the Verb: Does he know *what the price is?*
Subject: *What John said* is right.
Predicate Nominative: That is *what John told me.*

An Adjective Clause is a clause used as an adjective modifying a noun. It is introduced by the relative pronoun *who, whom, that, which.*

EXAMPLES:

The boy *who is reading the book* is Mary's brother.
The girl *whom she trusts* proved worthy of her confidence.
The dress *that I bought yesterday* was on sale.
The pencil *which lies upon the desk* is broken.

An Adverbial Clause modifies a verb, an adjective, or an adverb. It is introduced by such subordinating conjunctions as *after, although, as, because, before, if, since, until, when, than, whenever, where, while.*

EXAMPLES:

They did *as they were told.*

      (Modifies the verb *did*)

She is as intelligent *as he is.*

      (Modifies the adjective *intelligent*)

The goods were shipped earlier *than we expected.*

      (Modifies the adverb *earlier*)

Clauses and Phrases: The principal difference between a clause and a phrase is that a clause has a verb and a subject, and can stand alone as a sentence; whereas a phrase does not have a verb and a subject, and must depend on other parts of the sentence to complete its meaning.

PUNCTUATION

Proper punctuation in any sentence is as important as the proper arrangement of words. Punctuation marks are used to separate the structural units of the sentence and to bring out more clearly the writer's thought.

The style of punctuation used must be consistent and must be based on sentence structure. If the use of punctuation does not clarify the meaning, the chances are that the arrangement of words and ideas is at fault. Punctuation should help the reader to understand what he reads—*not* give him the wrong interpretation. Modern business correspondence demands precision, and proper punctuation helps to achieve this end.

For those concerned in the production of printed matter, as well as typewritten material, the *U.S. Government Printing Office Style Manual,* widely referred to throughout the nation, answers innumerable questions on style and good usage. Following are rules governing the use of punctuation.

PUNCTUATION SYMBOLS

The most frequently used punctuation symbols are:

1. Apostrophe   '   7. Parentheses ( )
2. Colon   :   8. Period .
3. Comma ,   9. Question Mark ?
4. Dash —   10. Quotation Marks " "
5. Exclamation Point ! 11. Semicolon ;
6. Hyphen -

THE APOSTROPHE

The apostrophe has a great many functions.

1. The most common use of the apostrophe is to indicate the possessive case of nouns and pronouns.

(a) To form the possessive case of a *singular noun,* add an apostrophe and an *s.*

EXAMPLES:

John's hat
boy's book

(b) To form the possessive case of a *plural noun* not ending in *s,* add an apostrophe and an *s.*

EXAMPLES:

men's shirts
children's games

(c) To form the possessive case of a *plural noun* ending in *s,* add the apostrophe *only.*

EXAMPLES:

boys' shoes
ladies' dresses

(d) The *indefinite pronouns* such as *one, everyone, everybody* form their possessive case in the same way as nouns.

EXAMPLES:

one's duty

everyone's opinion
everybody's concern

(e) To form the possessive of a compound noun, add the apostrophe and *s* at the end of the noun.

Example:

Mayor-elect's speech
sister-in-law's hat

Note: The plural of a compound noun is usually formed by adding *s* to the most important part of the compound. Thus: *sisters-in-law* is the nominative plural of *sister-in-law; sister-in-law's* is possessive singular; *sisters-in-law's* is possessive plural.

(f) Possessive pronouns such as the following do *not* take an apostrophe:

Example:

my, mine, your, yours, his, her, hers, their, theirs, your, yours, our, ours, whose, its
Note: Its is the possessive form of *it*. Never put an apostrophe in *its* unless you mean *it is*.

2. The apostrophe is used to indicate the omission of one or more letters in contractions or to denote the omission of figures from dates, as:

aren't (are not)	class of '64
it's (it is)	spirit of '76
I've (I have)	blizzard of '88

3. If two nouns indicate possession of the same thing, only the second is given the possessive form, while individual or alternative possession requires the use of an apostrophe on each element of a series.

EXAMPLES:

We buy at Brown & Nelson's store.
They sell men's, women's and children's clothing.

4. The apostrophe is used to indicate the coined plurals of letters, figures and symbols.

EXAMPLES:

Of letters: 4-H'ers; TV'ers; B.t.u.'s
                 three R's; a's, b's, c's; T's, Y's
Of figures: 7's, 8's, 9's
                 2 by 4's (lumber)
                 49'ers
                 but 10s (yarn and thread)
                       4½s (bonds)
                       3s (golf)
Of symbols: &'s, %'s, #'s, $'s, ¶'s

The plurals of abbreviations are often treated the same way:

EXAMPLES:

Read your A B C's.
Get their OK's first.
Here are two IOU's.

5. For easier pronunciation, nouns ending in *s* or *ce* and followed by a word beginning with *s* form the possessive by adding an apostrophe *only*.

EXAMPLES:

for goodness' sake
Mr. Hughes' service

for old times' sake
for acquaintance' sake
for conscience' sake

6. A noun preceding a gerund should be in the possessive case.

EXAMPLE:

In the event of <u>Mary's</u> <u>leaving</u>, you will sit here.
              /   /
          (Noun)   (Gerund)

7. A possessive noun used in an adjective sense requires the addition of *'s*.

EXAMPLES:

She is a friend of Jane's.
Macy's is running a sale.

8. The possessive case is often used in such expressions as the following, even though ownership is not involved.

EXAMPLES:

2 weeks' pay
1 day's labor (labor for 1 day)
a stone's throw
9 or 10 billion dollars' worth
2 hours' travel-time

9. The apostrophe is omitted in shortened forms of certain words, as: phone; coon; possum; Frisco; copter

10. The plural of spelled-out numbers, and of words referred to as words is formed by adding *s* or *es* instead of the apostrophe.

EXAMPLES:

Spelled-out numbers		*Words referred to as words*
ones, twos, threes	ins and outs	yeses and noes
sevens, eights, nines	ups and downs	whereases and wherefores

But the *'s* is added to indicate the plural of words used as words if the omission of the apostrophe would cause difficulty in reading.

EXAMPLES:

do's and don'ts	*not* dos and donts
which's and that's	*not* whichs and thats

THE COLON

The colon has the following principal uses:

1. A colon is used after the salutation in a letter or any written formal greeting.

EXAMPLES:

Dear Sir:
Gentlemen:
Dear Mr. Smith:
My dear Mr. Smith:
Dear Madam:
Ladies and Gentlemen:
To Whom It May Concern:

2. A colon is used between hours and minutes where the time is expressed in figures, as: 10:30 p.m.; 6:05 a.m.

Note 1: A colon is not used when no minutes follow the hour unless it is done for a specific purpose, as in tabulations: Thus: 10 p.m. (*not* 10:00 p.m.)

Note 2: To designate exact noon or exact midnight, the following forms are observed: 12 m. (noon); 12 p.m. (midnight)

Note 3: Other forms of expressing time are these: 10 o'clock (*not* 10 o'clock p.m.; *not* 2 p.m. in the afternoon); 6 hours 8 minutes 20 seconds; 7 minutes

3. A colon is placed after a statement that introduces a list of items, names or particulars.

EXAMPLES:

a. The following items were damaged during shipment:
   cup $ .60
   soup dish   1.25
   sugar bowl   1.75
b. The following people will attend the meeting:
   Mr. C. H. Smith
   Mr. H. V. Compton
   Mr. J. C. Dean
c. My work schedule as secretary in the sales department is as follows: I open the mail; take dictation; type estimates and schedules; and keep up with routine work.

4. A colon is used to separate the main title and the subtitle of a book.

EXAMPLES:

In Time of Sorrow: The Gift of Your Presence, by Seymour Shubin

New Guinea: The Land That Time Forgot, by Lowell Thomas

5. A colon is used before a quotation.

EXAMPLE:

Lincoln's Gettysburg Address: "Fourscore and seven years ago our fathers brought forth on this continent a new nation, conceived in liberty, and dedicated to the proposition that all men are created equal. Now we are engaged in a great civil war, testing . . ."

6. A colon is used between chapter and verse in a reference to the Bible.

EXAMPLE:

John 16: 16-22 (full space after colon)

7. The colon is used in imprints, such as:
U.S. Government Printing Office
Washington : 19—

Nihil Obstat: Arthur J. Scanlan, S.T.D., Censor Librorum. Imprimatur: Francis Cardinal Spellman, D.D., Archbishop of New York. August 24, 19—

THE COMMA

The *comma* is a mark of punctuation used to separate words, phrases, and clauses, and to indicate the smallest interruption in continuity of thought or grammatical construction.

Below are the principal functions of the comma:

Separating words and phrases.

1. A comma is used to separate a series of words except where they are joined by conjunctions.

EXAMPLE:

The report covered Aerospace, Business, Colleges and Universities, Electronics, Government Agencies, Labor, Military, Navy, Public Affairs, Transportation and United Nations.

2. Use a comma after each member of three or more words, phrases, letters or figures with *and, or,* or *nor.*

EXAMPLES:

The United States flag colors are red, white, *and* blue.
It is sold by the bolt, by the yard, *or* in remnants.
Neither snow, rain, *nor* heat stops the postman.
We drove 2 days, 3 hours, and 4 minutes.

3. A comma is used to separate a series of co-ordinate qualifying words.

EXAMPLES:

Outside the house is a well with *clear, cold water.*
Nearby is a brook with *cold, running water; but* The house is piped only with *running cold water.*

4. A comma is used to separate *adjectives* and *adverbs* in a series.

EXAMPLES:

A successful secretary is intelligent, adaptable, conscientious, observant, pleasant, and personable. (Adjectives)
Every secretary should perform her duties conscientiously, satisfactorily, carefully, skillfully, and artfully. (Adverbs)

5. A comma is used to separate a word or phrase in apposition (a word or expression placed next to another so that the second explains or identifies the first).

EXAMPLES:

Mason Jones, treasurer, read the minutes of last week's meeting.

Hamilton Smith, the guest of honor, spoke at the luncheon.

6. Use a comma to separate words in pairs of a series of phrases.

EXAMPLES:

Most of the artists work on lettering and layouts, folders and displays, packages and labels. (Words in pairs)

Their aim is to get the attention of the reader, hold his interest, arouse his desire for the product or service, get him to buy it, or perhaps just to recognize it. (Series of phrases)

7. A comma separates a word or phrase used in contrast to another.

EXAMPLE:

Our order dated June 4 called for a gross of labels, not ladles.

8. Use a comma to separate two words or figures that might otherwise be confusing.

EXAMPLES:

To Mary, Jane is a true friend.
Of the two, he is taller.
Instead of two, four came.
What the time is, is not certain; but they are going ahead with the plans for the luncheon.
Of 950, 500 copies were sold.
Read pages 25, 26, 27, 28.

9. Use a comma to indicate the omission of words that are understood in the sentence.

EXAMPLES:

                              wore   wore
                              /   /
Mary wore a red dress; Jane, a green dress; Ellen, a navy dress.

                         we have
                         /
Then we had much; now, nothing.

Separating clauses.

10. A comma is used to separate clauses in sentences where the participial construction is used.

EXAMPLES:

Seeing that it was impossibe to walk that far, I decided to take a bus.
Having done his homework, the boy went out to play.

11. Use a comma before the conjunction in a compound sentence with an independent clause.

EXAMPLES:

You will want to study their catalogs, *and* most schools are glad to answer your individual questions.
Pencils, pens, and office supplies are plentiful in most stationery stores, *and* many other labor-saving devices are also available.

12. Use a comma after an interrogative clause, followed by a direct question.

EXAMPLES:

You are going, are you not?
They will be there, will they not?

13. Use a comma to separate parenthetical expressions or those independent of the main thought of the sentence.

EXAMPLES:

So it is natural, when seeking people, that employers seek the best.
You may, however, obtain a position based on your knowledge and suitability for the job.

Separating direct quotations.

14. Use a comma to separate direct quotations unless followed by a question mark or exclamation point.

EXAMPLES:

The boy said, "I lost my book."
"We will help you find your book," his friends replied.
"Where did you lose it?" asked John.
"What a job we had to find it!" exclaimed Billy.

Separating titles, degrees, or abbreviations.

15. A comma is used between title of a person and the name of an organization in the absence of the words *of* or *of the*.

Examples:

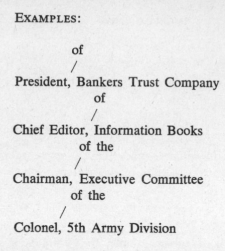

of
/
President, Bankers Trust Company

of
/
Chief Editor, Information Books

of the
/
Chairman, Executive Committee

of the
/
Colonel, 5th Army Division

16. A comma is used to separate, within a sentence, titles, degrees, or abbreviations *Jr., Sr., Esq., S.J.,* etc., from the names to which they belong.

Examples:

William Brown, Jr., president	(Title)
Henry Clay Smith, Ph.D.	(Degree)
William Brown, Sr.	(Abbreviation)
Malcolm Jones, Esq.	(Abbreviation)
Charles A. O'Neill, S.J.	(Abbreviation)
Washington, D.C.	(Abbreviation)

After the complimentary close of a letter.

17. A comma is used after the complimentary close of a letter.

Examples:

Sincerely,
Very truly yours,

Cordially yours,
Best regards,

Writing dates.
18. Use a comma after the year in complete dates within the sentence.

EXAMPLE:

On July 4, 1776, the Declaration of Independence was signed.

When the comma is omitted.
19. Do not use a comma between month and year in dates.

EXAMPLES:

July 1776
4th of July 1776
February and March 1969
January, February and March 1969
January 24 A.D. 1969
15th of June A.D. 1969
Labor Day 1969
Easter Sunday 1969

20. Do not use a comma before ZIP (zone improvement plan) postal-delivery number.

EXAMPLE:

New York, N.Y. 10017

21. Do not use a comma between two nouns one of which identifies the other.

EXAMPLE:

The Children's Bureau's *booklet* *"Infant Care"* is a best seller.
                         /   /
                       (Noun)   (Noun)

THE DASH

The dash has these functions:

1. The dash is used to indicate a break in thought or structure of a sentence.

EXAMPLE:

This department may consist of one man or woman, or an entire staff—depending upon the size of the company.

2. The dash is used to begin and end a parenthetical element (explanatory matter) within the sentence.

EXAMPLE:

But the great majority—and they were ten to one—overruled these objections.

3. The dash is used to indicate the omission of letters in a word.

EXAMPLE:

The troop, while crossing the desert, complained that the heat was hotter than h—l.

4. Where numbers have been omitted from a series or when denoting a period of time, the dash is frequently used in place of the word "to."

EXAMPLES:

The subject is discussed fully on pages 26-36. (Series)
Eisenhower was President of the United States during the years 1953-1961. (Denoting Time)
January-June is the period in question. (Denoting Time)
The clinic is open Monday-Friday during July and August. (Denoting Time)

5. The dash is used to set apart a statement or expression that is in apposition with the main thought.

EXAMPLE:

To prepare and place advertising—successful advertising for the advertiser—is the primary purpose of the advertising agency.

6. The dash is used after an introductory phrase that reads into the lines that follow and indicating repetition of the phrase.

EXAMPLE:

To be an accurate stenographer, it is suggested—
     That you listen carefully;
     That you get every word in shorthand outline; and
     That you transcribe your shorthand notes accurately
so that they will make sense.

7. The dash is sometimes used to denote an unfinished word or sentence.

EXAMPLES:

Patrick Henry said: "Give me lib—" (Unfinished Word)
He said: "I recall the time when—" (Unfinished Sentence)

The dash is not used—
1. When *and, between, from* and *to* are used with dates.

EXAMPLE:

From January 1 to June 30, 1969; *not* from January 1-June 30, 1969.
Between 1800 and 1900; *not* 1800-1900.

2. With the colon after the formal salutation of a letter.

EXAMPLE:

Dear Sir: *not* Dear Sir:—

EXCLAMATION POINT

Following are the rules for the use of the exclamation point:

1. An exclamation point is placed after an exclamatory word, phrase or sentence to show surprise or strong emotion.

EXAMPLES:

Alas! they arrived. (Exclamatory word)
If only you were here! (Exclamatory phrase)
Yes, I mean you! (Exclamatory sentence)

2. When the exclamation point is used at the end of an interrogative sentence that is interrogatory in form but exclamatory in meaning, the question mark is omitted.

EXAMPLES:

Should such conditions continue!
Who shouted, "Bravo!"

3. The exclamation point may be used after ironic statements.

EXAMPLE:

So you call this justice!

THE HYPHEN

1. The most common use of the hyphen is to mark the continuation of a word divided at the end of a line.

2. The hyphen is used between letters of spelled words.

EXAMPLE:

T-h-e-s-e a-r-e s-p-e-l-l-e-d w-o-r-d-s.

3. A hyphen is used to avoid doubling a vowel or tripling a consonant.

EXAMPLES:

micro-organism   brass-smith
semi-independent   shell-like

4. Print as one word compass directions consiting of two points of direction, but use a hyphen after the first point of direction when three points of direction are combined.

EXAMPLES:

northeast   north-northeast
southwest   south-southwest

5. The hyphen is used between the elements of compound

numerals from *twenty-one* to *ninety-nine;* also from *twenty-first* to *ninety-ninth.*

6. The hyphen is ofen used between the elements of a fraction, but omit it when the hyphen appears in either or both.

EXAMPLES:

one-thousandth   twenty-three thirtieths
two-thirds   twenty-one thirty-seconds
two one-thousandths   three-fourths of an inch
four-fifths

7. A hyphen is used in *adjective compounds* with a numerical first element.

EXAMPLES:

6-footer   20th-century progress
24-inch ruler   3-to-1 ratio
3-week vacation   5-to-4 vote
8-hour day   2-cent-per-pound tax
10-minute delay   two-sided question

8. Some compound names indicating family relationships are printed with a hyphen; some are printed as one word, some as two words.

EXAMPLES:

mother-in-law   stepson
great-grandmother   stepbrother
great-grandchild   half brother
great-granddaughter   first cousin
great-grandson   second cousin

9. The hyphen is used between the elements of technical compound units of measurement.

EXAMPLES:

kilowatt-hour   light-year
horsepower-hour   passenger-mile

10. Combination color terms are usually printed as separate words, except when such color terms are unit modifiers.

EXAMPLES:

Its feathers are *bluish green*.
It has *bluish-green* feathers.

When the hyphen is omitted—

11. Print without a hyphen a two-word modifier, the first element of which is a comparative or a superlative.

EXAMPLES:

Comparative	*Superlative*
better paying job	best liked book
higher level decision	highest priced apartment
lower income group	most read advertisement
but lowercase, uppercase (printing)	*but* bestseller (noun)

12. Do not use a hyphen in a unit modifier consisting of a foreign phrase, as: bona fide transaction; per capita tax; per diem employee.

PARENTHESES

1. Parentheses are used to set off matter not intended to be

part of the main thought or not a grammatical element of the sentence.

EXAMPLES:

The result (see footnote) is most surprising.

The signature of a business letter consists usually of the name of the writer and his business title (if he has one).

2. Parentheses are used to enclose numbered or lettered items in a paragraph.

EXAMPLES:

Business writing has two functions: (1) to inform and (2) to influence.

The functions of business writing are: (a) to inform, (b) to influence.

3. A parenthetical reference at the end of a sentence is placed *before* the period, unless it is a complete sentence in itself.

EXAMPLES:

Now let us analyze the following items (33 to 40).

(See also items 50 to 60.)

4. Parentheses are used to enclose a figure inserted to confirm a statement given in words, if double form is specifically desired.

EXAMPLE:

Payment is due in sixty (60) days.

THE PERIOD

The period has these functions:

1. A period marks the end of a complete declarative sentence, an imperative sentence, or an indirect question intended as a suggestion and not requiring an answer.

EXAMPLES:

He walks to school every day. (Declarative)
Stop where you are. (Imperative)
May we hear from you regarding shipment. (Indirect question)

2. If a declarative sentence ends with an abbreviation, only one period is used—*not* one for the abbreviation and one for the end of the sentence.

EXAMPLES:

The books will be sent C.O.D.
The pages are numbered one, two, three, etc.

3. The period, however, *cannot* take the place of any other punctuation symbol.

EXAMPLES:

Will the books be sent C.O.D.?
He will say it everytime!

4. A period follows most abbreviations and initials.

EXAMPLES:

N.Y.   gal.   J.C. Doe

5. If an abbreviation is used within the sentence, its period is followed by any other punctuation symbol that the sense of the sentence requires.

EXAMPLES:

If the meeting is at 2 p.m., I will be able to attend.
The books arrived C.O.D.; so I paid for them.

6. A period precedes a decimal fraction.

EXAMPLES:

3.25 percent $1.50   1.25 meters

7. The period is used in place of parentheses after a letter or number denoting a series.

EXAMPLES:

a. _____   1. _____
b. _____   2. _____
c. _____   3. _____

8. When indicating main divisions and subdivisions in an outline, place the period after letters or figures except when they are enclosed in parentheses.

EXAMPLES:

I.   (main division)
    A.   (first subdivision)
    B.   (first subdivision)
    C.   (first subdivision)
        1.   (second subdivision)
        2.   (second subdivision)

a.	(third subdivision)
b.	(third subdivision)
c.	(third subdivision)
(1)	(fourth subdivision)
(2)	(fourth subdivision)
(a)	(fifth subdivision)
(b)	(fifth subdivision)

II. etc.
III. etc.
IV. etc.

The period is omitted in the following instances:

9. After—
   Titles of manuscripts.
   Headings for articles or chapters of a book.
   Tabular column headings.
   Scientific, chemical or other symbols.

Note: This rule does *not* apply to periods after abbreviations.

EXAMPLE:

Functions of S.P.C.A.

10. After a quotation mark that is preceded by a period.

EXAMPLE:

He said, "Be there on time."

11. After a short name which is not an abbreviation of the longer form.

EXAMPLE:

Ben (Benjamin)   Ed (Edward)   Will (William)

12. After Roman numerals used as ordinals (*first, second, third,* etc.) in distinction from (*one, two, three,* etc.).

Henry I   Elizabeth II   George III

Note: If the Roman numerals fall at the end of the sentence, then the period is added:

EXAMPLE:

The proclamation was issued by George III.

QUESTION MARK

1. The question mark is used at the end of all interrogative sentences that ask a direct question.

EXAMPLES:

Where is your hat?
What is your name?

Note: After an indirect question use a period instead of a question mark. (See Rule 1 under The Period.)

2. The question mark may be used to separate more than one question in the same sentence.

EXAMPLE:

Can we depend on his ability? his knowledge? his fortitude?

3. The question mark may be used to express doubt.

EXAMPLE:

Lincoln was born in 1800(?) and died in 1865.

4. The question mark is placed *inside* the quotation mark if the quotation is a question.

EXAMPLE:

I asked the pilot, "How fast are we flying?"

5. If the whole sentence is a question, the question mark is placed *outside* the quotation mark.

EXAMPLE:

Did I hear him say, "five hundred miles an hour"?

QUOTATION MARKS

1. The quotation mark is used to enclose direct quotations. (*Note:* Each part of an interrupted quotation begins and ends with quotation marks.)

EXAMPLES:

The inspector said, "No trespassing is allowed. This is private property."
"What right have you," he asked, "to cut down the timber?"

2. Do not use quotation marks or capital letters in indirect quotations.

EXAMPLES:

Tell Jane yes.
She could not say no.

3. Quotation marks are used at the beginning of each paragraph of a quotation but at the end of only the last paragraph.

Example:

"_____
_____
_____.
"_____
_____
_____.
"_____
_____
_____
_____."

4. Titles of books, magazine articles, stories, songs, motion pictures, plays, operas, poems, and other titles are usually enclosed in quotation marks, although they are sometimes underlined instead.

(*Note:* The device of underlining is commonly used in manuscripts by writers whose material is to appear in printed form. It is simply their note to the printer that they want such titles or certain words italicized. The reason for the underlining is that they cannot write or typewrite in *italics.*)

5. When the quotation mark appears with other marks of punctuation:

a. The *period* and the *comma* usually precede the ending quotation mark.

Examples:

He said, "Here they come."
"Here they come," he said.

b. The *colon* and *semicolon* are usually placed after the ending quotation mark.

EXAMPLES:

"Gone With The Wind": a bestseller, is read the world over.
He said, "Bixby was to be a sort of brother-in-law of Bromley's"; he was to marry Mrs. Bromley's half sister.

c. The *exclamation point* and *question mark* are usually placed *inside* the quotation mark when they are part of the quoted material, or *after* when they refer to the whole sentence.

EXAMPLES:

He said "Surprise!" and walked away.
He asked, "Is this Grand Central Station?"
What a queer way to say "Surprise"!
Did he say "Next stop"?

SEMICOLON

The *semicolon* is used to indicate a more distinct separation between parts of a sentence than that indicated by a comma.
Following are the principal functions of the semicolon:

1. The semicolon is used to separate clauses containing commas.

EXAMPLES:

a. Malcolm Jones, president of Jones & Jones Company, was also a director of ABC Tool Company; Harvey W. Smith, chairman of the Board of Endicott & Co., was also on the board of Amalgamated Steel Co.

b. We welcome comparison because this policy pays from the first day, we can't pay any sooner; it pays forever, we can't pay any longer.

c. Yes, sir; he will come.

d. No, sir; I do not recall.

2. The semicolon separates statements that are too closely related in meaning to be written as separate sentences, and also statements of contrast.

EXAMPLES:

a. *Closely related in meaning.*
Yes; it is so.
No; we sold half.
There are no strings attached; you are under no obligation.

b. *Statements of contrast.*
It is true in peace; it is true in war.
War is destructive; peace, constructive.
Some are regional in scope; others have national coverage.

3. The semicolon is used to set off explanatory abbreviations (*i.e., e.g., viz.*) or words which summarize or explain preceding matter (*namely, that is*).

EXAMPLES:

a. The industry is related to groups that produce finished goods; i.e., electrical machinery and transportation equipment.
b. There were involved three metal producers; namely, Jones & Laughlin, Armco, and Kennecott.

Note: The semicolon is to be avoided where a comma will suffice.

EXAMPLE:

Regional offices are located in New York, N.Y., Chicago, Ill., and Dallas, Texas.

CAPITALIZATION

A capital letter is any letter written or printed in a form larger than, and often different from, that of the corresponding small letters. Examples: A, B, C, D (uppercase letters); a, b, c, d (lowercase letters).

Capital letters are used primarily for the beginnings of sentences and for proper names. There are many other uses regarding capital letters. However, it is impossible to give all the rules that will cover every conceivable problem in capitalization. But if we consider the purpose to be served and the underlying principles, it is possible that a considerable degree of uniformity will be attained.

Following are rules set by the *U.S. Government Printing Office Style Manual* on the use of capitals:

1. First Words.
Capitalize the first word—

EXAMPLES:

Of a sentence
We will ship your order early in May.
Of an independent clause or phrase
The question is, Will you deliver the order on time?
Of a direct quotation
He asked, "Can you deliver the desk this week?"
Of an expression that stands for a sentence
Impossible! The desk is expected to arrive from the factory next week.

Of a line of poetry
> Twinkle, twinkle, little star,
> > How I wonder what you are.

After a colon when it introduces a complete sentence having independent meaning
> A first precept of intelligent newspaper reading therefore is: Be wary of any controversial statement when no source for it is set forth.

Do not capitalize the first word—

EXAMPLES:

Of a quotation resumed within a sentence
> "What I need," said a busy executive, "is a secretary who can assume responsibility."

Of a fragmentary quotation
> Your cooperation is, as he said, "absolutely essential."
> They objected "to the phraseology, not to the ideas."

After a semicolon
> It sounds like a simple thing to do; actually it is extremely difficult.

After a colon if the matter following is merely a supplementary remark making the meaning clearer.
> Railroading is not a variety of outdoor sport: it is service.

2. Proper Names.

Capitalize all proper names, including nicknames; names of holidays; geographical names; names of buildings, organizations and institutions; names of governmental agencies, departments, and high-ranking officials; names of historical documents and events; words of kinship; and names of races and languages.

EXAMPLES:

John Smith	Smithsonian Institution
Ike Eisenhower	Federal Bureau of Investigation
Easter Sunday	the Chief Justice
Mississippi River	Declaration of Independence
Empire State Building	Uncle Charlie
United Nations Building	Indian
Ford Foundation	Spanish

3. Derivatives of proper names.

Derivatives of proper names used with a proper meaning are capitalized.

EXAMPLES:

Roman (of Rome)	German (of Germany)
Italian (of Italy)	English (of England)

Derivatives of proper names used with acquired independent common meaning, or no longer identified with such names, are usually lowercased.

EXAMPLES:

alaska seal (fur)	french dressing
brazil nut	german silver
castile soap	india ink
chinese blue	japan varnish
dotted swiss	kraft paper

4. Names of regions, localities, and geographic features.

(a) Capitalize a descriptive term used to denote a definite region, locality, or geographic feature.

EXAMPLES:

the Gulf States	the Far East
North Central States	the East
Far Western States	the North Pole
the West	the North and South Poles
Deep South	the East Side (section of a city)

(b) A descriptive term used to denote mere direction or position is not a proper name and is therefore not capitalized.

EXAMPLES:

east; easterly; eastern; eastward
west; westerly; western; westward
north; northerly; northern; northward
south; southerly; southern; southward
eastern region; western region; north-central region
east coast; eastern seaboard; west coast, western seaboard

(c) Terms denoting time are as follows:

Atlantic	local
Atlantic standard	local standard
central standard	mountain standard
eastern	Pacific
eastern daylight	Pacific standard
eastern standard	universal

5. *Titles of persons.*

Capitalize any title or designation immediately preceding a name.

EXAMPLES:

President Nixon	Lieutenant Briggs
Ambassador Jones	Chairman Donavan

Professor McMahon	Nurse Payne
King Louis	Judge Samuel

A common-noun title immediately following the name of a person or used alone as a substitute for it is usually capitalized to indicate preeminence or distinction in certain specified instances such as:

Title of a head or assistant head of state:

EXAMPLES:

Richard M. Nixon, President of the United States:
    the President
    the President-elect
    the Executive
    the Chief Magistrate
    the Commander in Chief
    ex-President Eisenhower
    former President Truman
Similarly:
    the Vice President
    the Vice-President-elect
    ex-Vice-President Humphrey
Nelson A. Rockefeller, Governor of New York:
    the Governor of New York
    the Governor
Similarly:
    the Lieutenant Governor
But:
    secretary of state of New York
    attorney general of New York

Titles of members of diplomatic corps:
Walter S. Gifford, Ambassador Extraordinary and Plenipotentiary:
    the American Ambassador

the British Ambassador
the Ambassador
the Senior Ambassador
Similarly:
the Envoy Extraordinary and Minister Plenipotentiary:
the Envoy
the Minister
the Chargé d'Affaires
the Chargé
Ambassador at Large
Minister Without Portfolio
But:
the consul general
the consul
the attaché

Title of a ruler or prince:
Elizabeth II, Queen of England:
the Queen
the Crown
Her Most Gracious Majesty
Her Majesty
Similarly:
the Emperor
the Sultan
Edward, Prince of Wales:
the Prince
His Royal Highness

A title in the second or third person is capitalized.

EXAMPLES:

Mr. Chairman
Mr. Secretary
Your Excellency

Your Highness
Your Honor

6. *Religious Terms.*
Capitalize all words denoting Deity except *who, whose,* and *whom;* all names for the Bible and other sacred writings; all names of religious bodies and their adherents and words specifically denoting Satan.

EXAMPLES:

Heavenly Father; the Almighty; Thee; Thou; He; Him; Divine Father; Son of Man; the Messiah; Bible; Holy Scriptures; Scriptures; Koran; Biblical; Scriptural; Gospel (memoir of Christ); Episcopal Church; an Episcopalian; Catholicism; a Protestant; Christian; Christianity; Black Friars; Brother(s); King's Daughters; Daughter(s); Ursuline Sisters; Sister(s); Satan; the Devil; Father of Lies.

Do not capitalize: himself; (God's) fatherhood; divine providence; divine guidance; divine service; a messiah; messiahship; messianic; messianize; christology; christological; gospel truth; a devil; the devils.

7. *Scientific names.*
The words *sun, moon,* and *earth* are capitalized only if they are used in association with the names of other astronomical bodies that are capitalized.

EXAMPLE:

The nine planets orbiting the Sun are Mercury, Venus, Earth, Mars, Jupiter, Saturn, Uranus, Neptune, and Pluto. The Moon is Earth's satellite.

8. *Titles of publications, papers, documents, acts, laws, etc.*
The first word and all important words are capitalized in full

or short titles of annual reports, historic documents, legal cases, periodicals, and works of art.

EXAMPLES:

Annual Report of the Radin Company (*Note:* tenth annual report; 10th annual report)
Declaration of Independence; the Declaration (short title)
United States v. Morgan Jamison (legal case)
Journal of Arts and Sciences (periodical)
The Blue Boy (painting)

9. *Trades Names.*
Trade names, variety names, and names of market grades and brands are capitalized.

EXAMPLES:

Kodak (trade name)
Red Radiance rose (variety name)
Choice beef (market grade)

10. *Calendar divisions.*
The names of the days of the week and months of the year are capitalized.

EXAMPLES:

January; February; March; etc.
Monday; Tuesday; Wednesday; etc.
(*Note:* Do not capitalize the names of the seasons; spring, summer, autumn (fall), winter, unless they are personified, as in poetry: Autumn's golden charm; Winter's icy chill.)

11. *Salutations.*
Capitalize the first word of the salutation and all proper names and titles.

EXAMPLES:

Dear Mr. Smith:
Dear Dr. and Mrs. Jamison:
Dear John:
My dear Mrs. Compton:
(*Note: Do not capitalize* the word *dear* following the pronoun My.)

12. *Addresses.*

(a) Examples of general addresses when not followed by a salutation. (Note the use of colon at end of line.)

To Whom It May Concern:
To the Congress of the United States:
Collectors of Customs:
To the American Diplomatic and Consular Officers:

(b) Examples illustrating other types of addresses:
To the Director:
To the Editor:
To the Clerk of the House of Representatives:

15. *Complimentary Closes.*

Capitalize only the first word of the complimentary close in a letter.

EXAMPLES:

Very truly yours,
Sincerely yours,
Respectfully yours,

NUMERALS

Following are rules governing the use of numerals.

1. Fractions standing alone, or if followed by the words *of a* or *of an,* are generally spelled out.

EXAMPLES:

one half a lot	one hundredth
a quarter of an inch	two one-hundredths
three-quarters of an inch	one half an inch

2. Round numbers are spelled out:

EXAMPLES:

a hundred dollars
a thousand dollars
a million and a half
less than a million dollars

3. Numbers larger than 1,000, if spelled out, should be in the following form:

EXAMPLES:

two thousand and twenty
one thousand five hundred and fifty
one hundred and twenty-five thousand two hundred and ten

4. A unit of measurement, time, or money is always expressed in figures.

EXAMPLES:

He walked a 1-mile road to work.

A team of four men ran the 1-mile relay in 3 minutes 10 seconds.

He was paid 75 cents an hour.

5. Numbers expressing time, money, or measurement separated from their unit descriptions by more than two words are spelled out if under 10.

EXAMPLES:

two *and more separate* years
whether five *or any number of* years

6. Usually a number less than 10 is spelled out within a sentence.

EXAMPLES:

The six pencils are on the desk.
This space is three times as wide as that space.

7. A spelled-out number should not be repeated in figures except in legal documents, such as:
   five (5) dollars, *not* five dollars 5
   ten dollars ($10), *not* ten ($10) dollars

ACCURATE SPELLING

Few people are proficient spellers. One of the reasons there are so many poor spellers among educated people is that they seem to think the subject of spelling is not of sufficient importance to warrant careful study.

Correct spelling is absolutely essential for business communication. An indispensable requisite for every secretary who aspires to be a good secretary is that she be able to spell. If she can't spell correctly, she is in trouble. Her inability to spell may either keep her from getting the job she wants or prevent her from rising in her chosen field.

Learning to spell involves concentration, discipline, and hard work. A good memory certainly aids in the process of learning. It is almost impossible to know how to spell every word correctly; but applying spelling rules is one approach to correct spelling.

Six Rules To Spell Correctly

You can attain greater proficiency in spelling by:
1. Seeing a word correctly.
2. Pronouncing a word correctly.
3. Studying the order and arrangement of the letters that form a word and keeping the image of the word in your mind.
4. Learning the fundamental rules of spelling.
5. Spelling carefully to avoid errors.
6. Consulting a dictionary when in doubt.

Prefixes and Suffixes Which Cause Difficulty

Words beginning with the prefixes *extra-, non-, over-, re-, ultra-* often cause difficulty in spelling. These words may be found in a good dictionary specially listed under their respective alphabetical sequence.

1. *Words Ending in -Able.*

-Able, a suffix meaning *able to,* is used in forming adjectives from nouns and verbs, principally verbs, such as: person + able (noun root); work + able (verb root). Some other examples are absorbable, acceptable, remarkable.

Other *-able* words are formed by dropping the *E* or *Y* (with *E* sound) from the root word, as in mistakable, reputable, solvable, miserable; or formed from words ending in *-ate,* such as appreciable, separable, tolerable; or from Latin roots, such as amenable, durable, or unpalatable.

2. *Words Ending in -Ible.*

-Ible is a variable of *able* used in forming adjectives derived from Latin verbs ending in *-ire* or *-ere,* as the following: accessible, digestible, discernible, flexible, visible.

3. *Words Ending in -Ally, -Ly.*

-Ally is an adverbial suffix added to certain adjectives with stems in *-ic* which have no forms ending in *ical,* as: frantic + ally=frantically. Other examples are academically, emphatically, fantastically, systematically.

-Ly is an adverbial suffix used to indicate a specific manner or point of view, as: slow+ly=slowly; part+ly=partly. Other examples are: badly, candidly, infinitely, tremblingly.

If the adjective ends in *l, ly* is added to complete the root, thus producing an *lly* ending as in accidentally, actually, usually, woefully.

4. *Words Ending in -Ance, -Ence, -Ar, -Er, and -Or.*

Many spelling errors occur when there is carelessness in the use of the *-ance, -ence, -ar, -er,* and *-or* endings. So many words are involved that the best thing to do is to consult your dictionary frequently until you have memorized most of these problem words.

Chapter 8

HOW TO GET
HELPFUL REFERENCE
INFORMATION QUICKLY
AND EASILY

SOURCES OF INFORMATION

An excellent rule to follow in your work is:

Don't guess, know where to find the answers.

Occasionally, questions arise which are beyond your knowledge and that of others in your office. These questions may relate to the spelling of a word or name, a statistic, a custom, or a regulation. Rather than guess, you can find the answer quickly and easily. All you need to do is take the time to look it up.

The factual information which business organizations use *must* be accurate. When you are called on to track down facts, your executive expects you to be able to find the information he needs; and to find it, you must know *where* to look it up. One of the best guides to all sources of information is: *How and*

Where to Look It Up by Robert W. Murphey (McGraw-Hill Book Company, Inc., publishers, New York, Toronto, London). This book tells you where to find the data you are seeking. It lists under appropriate headings the most useful sources in hundreds of different fields or subjects. From it you can choose quickly the most logical source to meet your needs. This book and many reference books are or should be readily available in your company or local library. Other sources of references should also be available in your own office, if only in the form of pocket editions.

A good many questions can best be answered by a telephone call. If you need an unusual piece of information right away, and it is not readily available in your desk books or company library, try calling your local newspaper. Most large newspapers have a regular reference section which gives out free information. Also, the United States Department of Commerce offers a complete coverage of business information. Try your local Department of Commerce office.

Three basic reference books should always be on your desk or nearby, ready for instant use. They are a dictionary, a thesaurus, and a telephone directory.

DICTIONARY

A good dictionary can be the handiest book in your office. It is a guide to correct word usage just as a good map is a guide of the earth's terrain. The dictionary is a record of the English language. In it may be found: (1) the meaning of a word; (2) how to spell a word; (3) how to hyphenate a word or divide a word at the end of the line; (4) how to pronounce a word; (5) what part of speech it is; (6) its etymological derivation or some important fact of its usage.

In addition to giving the etymology and formation of words, a good dictionary contains much valuable information, such as:

—the names of Colleges and Universities of the United States;
—the names of Junior Colleges of the United States;

—the names of major foreign Colleges and Universities;

—proper forms of address in greeting some distinguished Americans;

—standard forms of abbreviations;

—tables of Weights and Measures;

—special Signs and Symbols pertaining to Astronomy, Biology, Chemistry, Commerce and Finance, Mathematics, Medicine, as well as Miscellaneous signs;

—major dates and events in world history;

—geographical statistics;

—standard time in various places throughout the world.

The above items vary according to the size of the book. Because the dictionary contains such a wealth of factual information, it has become a valuable tool to scholars, specialists, editors, speakers, business executives, as well as to secretaries. Some secretaries, however, fail to realize how helpful the dictionary can be, especially when they want to know how to spell a word. Rather than look it up, they prefer to ask other secretaries how to spell it. This is wrong. In the first place, they annoy the other workers by shouting out across the office. In the second place, they are less likely to remember the correct spelling that way. The fact is, when we hear something, we are more likely to forget it than when we actually see it.

Whenever you want to know how to spell a word, don't rely on your memory or on that of your fellow-workers—look it up yourself! By seeing it, you will learn how to spell it correctly . . . how to pronounce it . . . what part of speech it is . . . how to divide it at the end of the line . . . you will even learn its etymological derivation, if it has one. But more importantly, you will *remember* it.

Some good dictionaries:

The American College Dictionary. New York: Random House

Funk & Wagnalls Standard College Dictionary. New York: Funk & Wagnalls, a Division of Reader's Digest Books, Inc.

The Random House Dictionary of the English Language (Unabridged) New York: Random House

Webster's New World Dictionary of the American Language (College Edition). Cleveland and New York: The World Publishing Company

Webster's Third New International Dictionary (Unabridged) Springfield, Mass.: G. & C. Merriam Company, Publishers

THESAURUS

When you find yourself repeating words or phrases in your conversations or in your letters and reports, the thesaurus will end your word troubles. It will expand your knowledge of words and help to enrich your vocabulary.

What is a thesaurus? The *thesaurus* is a treasury of synonyms and antonyms. It is not a dictionary which gives the meanings of words. The thesaurus is a valuable tool in business and social life that will help you find the words that express your ideas most exactly. It will show you how to use words according to their precise shades of meaning.

The thesaurus is a wonderful aid to acquiring a command of words for better self-expression. As an example, let us assume you are describing a sunset. The first word that comes to your mind is "beautiful." Rather than bore your reader or listener by repeating the word several times, suppose you try to find some synonyms. This problem can best be solved with a thesaurus.

1. Turn to the index in the second half of your thesaurus. (*Roget's International Thesaurus.* Thomas Y. Crowell Company, publishers, New York; or *Roget's Pocket Thesaurus,* published by Pocket Books, Inc., New York)

2. Now look up the word "beautiful" which is listed alphabetically. In *Roget's Pocket Thesaurus,* this is the way it appears:

beautiful 845

3. Next, go to the first half of the book, which is set up numerically from 1-1000. Turn to the 800 section until you come to 845, which appears alongside the word "beauty." There you will find words grouped under such headings, as nouns, verbs, adjectives. Since the word "beautiful" is an adjective, you will be concerned with the adjectives. This is the way they appear:

> *Adj.* beautiful, beauteous, handsome, pretty, lovely, graceful, elegant, brilliant, exquisite, delicate, shining, sparkling, radiant, splendid, superb, resplendent, dazzling, glowing, magnificent, gorgeous

You have just discovered twenty words that may possibly be used in place of the word "beautiful." You know, of course, that every word won't express your idea precisely. After analyzing each word for its exact shade of meaning, you finally come up with the following:

> brilliant, exquisite, radiant, dazzling, glowing, magnificent

Now, let us assume you desire to expand your vocabulary.

1. Turn to the index in the second half of your thesaurus and look up the word "brilliant." This is the way it appears:

brilliant shining 420
witty 842
beautiful 845
glorious 873

2. Next, turn to 420 in the 400 section of the first half of your thesaurus, and you will find the following adjectives for the word "shining":

> vivid, luminous, lucent, bright, aglow

3. Now, look up the word "vivid" in the alphabetical section. This is the way it appears:

vivid bright 420, 428

4. Next, skip 420 (you already looked it up) and turn to 428 in the first half of the book. The following adjectives appear for the word "vivid": intense, deep, rich, bright-colored.

So far, you have found six more words that can help express your idea of a sunset more exactly and more vividly. They are:

vivid, luminous, lucent, bright, aglow, bright-colored

Repeat this same process whenever you need synonyms for other words. You'll be amazed how quickly and easily you can expand and enrich your vocabulary. The thesaurus is a wonderful aid for everyone who wants to speak and write effectively. Once you've used a thesaurus, you won't want to be without one.

TELEPHONE DIRECTORY

Your telephone directory can be just as handy as your dictionary. In addition to giving you addresses and telephone numbers, your telephone directory also shows you the correct spelling of firm names and people. If you are writing to an individual for the first time, it creates a bad impression to misspell his name or his firm's name. Consult your telephone directory whenever you are in doubt regarding such details. Your telephone directory also contains complete listings of United States Government, State, and City departments and agencies. Frequently called numbers are grouped in dark type at the beginning of each listing.

The Yellow Pages, another helpful source of information, consists basically of listings of business names, addresses, and telephone numbers under appropriate headings of businesses, products, professions, trades, and services. A Quick Reference

Index listed alphabetically at the beginning of your Yellow Pages is designed to help you find the product or service you are looking for; Yellow Pages Headings are printed in the Index in dark type. For example, if you should need a new office file cabinet, turn to the *Quick Reference Index.* Under "Office System" is this heading:

See Filing Equip Systems & Supls

Next, turn to the heading *Filing Equip., Systems & Supls.* in the listings section. There you will find arranged alphabetically the names of various firms which specialize in office furniture. In addition to a name listing, most firms or persons advertise in the Yellow Pages because they want you to call them. For that reason, many listings give detailed information.

Other sources can be very helpful whenever you need information.

ADVERTISING

Printers' Ink Advertisers' Guide to Marketing. New York: Printers' Ink Publishing Co.

Standard Advertising Register. New York: National Register Publishing Co., Inc.

Standard Rate and Data Service. Chicago: Standard Rate and Data Service, Inc.

ALMANACS

Information Please Almanac. Planned and supervised by Dan Golenpaul Associates. New York: (publisher varies)

Whitaker's Almanack by Joseph Whitacker. London House

The World Almanac and Book of Facts. (Annual) New York: Newspaper Enterprise Association, Inc.

ATLASES

Encyclopaedia Britannica World Atlas. Chicago: Encyclopaedia Britannica, Inc.

Rand McNally Commercial Atlas and Marketing Guide. Chicago: Rand McNally & Company

Rand McNally Pocket World Atlas. New York: Pocket Books, Inc.

Rand McNally World Atlas. Chicago: Rand McNally & Company

TWA Vacation Guide and World Atlas. Maplewood, N.J.: C. S. Hammond and Co.

BUSINESS AND FINANCIAL INFORMATION

Business

Business Statistics. U.S. Department of Commerce. Washington, D.C.: Government Printing Office

Business Executives of America. New York: Institute for Research in Biography, Inc.

Poor's Register of Directors and Executives, United States and Canada. New York: Standard and Poor's Corporation

Reference Book of Dun and Bradstreet, Inc. New York: Dun and Bradstreet, Inc.

Financial

Handbook of Commercial, Financial and Information Services. New York: Special Libraries Association

Moody's Stock Survey. New York: Moody's Investors Service

The Interpretation of Financial Statements. New York: Harper & Row, Publishers

Government

Official Congressional Directory. Washington, D.C.: United States Government Printing Office

Official Register of the U.S. Government. U.S. Civil Service Commission. Washington, D.C.: Government Printing Office

The Statesman's Year-Book. New York: St. Martin's Press, Inc.

United States Government Organization Manual. Washington, D.C.: Government Printing Office

INDEXES TO PERIODICALS

Art Index. New York: The H. W. Wilson Company

Industrial Arts Index. New York: The H. W. Wilson Company

New York Times Index. New York: New York Times

Readers' Guide to Periodical Literature. New York: The H. W. Wilson Company

NEWSPAPERS

N. W. Ayer and Son's Directory of Newspapers and Periodicals. Philadelphia: N. W. Ayer and Son, Inc.

Editor and Publisher: International Yearbook Number. New York: Editor and Publisher

Editor & Publisher Market Guide. New York: Editor & Publisher Co., Inc.

The Literary Market Place. New York: R. R. Bowker Company

PERSONS

Who's Who. (Annual biographical dictionary) New York: St. Martin's Press

Who's Who Among Association Executives. New York: Institute for Research in Biography, Inc.

Who's Who in America. Chicago: Who's Who, Inc. (The A. N. Marquis Co.)

Who's Who in Commerce and Industry. Chicago: The A. N. Marquis Company

Who's Who in the East. Chicago: The A. N. Marquis Company

Who's Who in the West. Chicago: The N. W. Marquis Company

POSTAL INFORMATON

Directory of Post Offices. U.S. Post Office Department. Washington, D.C.: Government Printing Office

National Zip Code Directory. A publication of the Post Office Department. Washington, D.C.: Government Printing Office

Postal Manual. U.S. Post Office. Washington, D.C.: Government Printing Office

STYLE MANUALS

New York Times Style Book. New York: New York Times Publishing Co.

United States Government Printing Office Style Manual. Washington, D.C.: Government Printing Office

FORMS OF ADDRESS, SALUTATION, COMPLIMENTARY CLOSE

Forms of address, salutation, and complimentary close are determined by social and official custom. There are many optional variations in forms of address, especially in the salutation and complimentary close.

In addressing distinguished Americans and people of other nationalities the proper form of address is to be ascertained and the correct title used. The forms of American address follow the general practice of the United States Department of State.

For the correct titles in general of American officials, and for a complete list of government agencies, see the *Congressional Directory,* the *United States Government Organization Manual,* the *Biographic Register of the Department of State,* and the Military Service registers.

Consult standard works of reference for the correct titles in general of foreign heads of states, members of the nobility, and foreign diplomats and officials. For the correct British titles, see the *Colonial Office List,* the *Foreign Office List, The Statesman's Year-Book, Whitaker's Almanack,* and *Whitaker's Peerage.*

Regarding forms for ceremonial diplomatic communications, such as letters of credence, recall, full powers, etc., see Satow, *A Guide to Diplomatic Practice.* Complimentary titles of address are generally written in full in diplomatic correspondence. See *Diplomatic List* for correct address.

In addressing high officials in general, distinctions in complimentary titles of address are to be observed:

1. The use of *Excellency* in addressing American officials is not an American custom. *His Excellency* is the complimentary diplomatic title used in addressing a foreign president, a foreign ambassador, a foreign cabinet officer, a foreign high official, or a former high official. *His Excellency* is used in the address; *Excellency* is used in the salutation and, generally, in the complimentary close; and *Your Excellency* is used in the body of the communication.

2. *Honorable,* written in full and always preceded by *The* (*the*) is used in addressing *by name* high officials and former high officials of the American government, foreign ministers (including a career minister serving as chargé d'affaires), and heads of international organizations, unless entitled to *His Excellency* by reason of a position previously held.

A person once entitled to *His Excellency* or *The Honorable* continues to be so addressed. However, it is customary to omit such title when addressing the Prime Minister or a cabinet officer or a member of the British Commonwealth of Nations.

3. *Esquire,* generally written in full in American diplomatic correspondence, is preferably used after the names of: (a) Foreign Service officers below the grade of career ministers; (b) Clerk of the Supreme Court of the United States; (c) officers of other courts.

4. *Dr.* (abbreviated before a name) is used in addressing persons who have acquired entitling degrees, but should not be used in combination with the abbreviations indicating such degrees.

EXAMPLES:

Dr. Smith
Dr. James Smith
James Smith, M.D. *not* Dr. James Smith, M.D.
James Smith, Ph.D. *not* Dr. James Smith, Ph.D.

5. *Reverend, Right Reverend,* etc., written in full and preceded by *The(the),* are used in addressing members of the clergy or episcopate.

EXAMPLES:

The(the) Reverend James Carter (clergyman)
The(the) Right Reverend James Carter (bishop)
The(the) Reverend Mr.(Dr.) Carter
The(the) Reverend Carter (with surname only) is *not* correct form.
Note: The article *the* when preceding *Reverend* in a sentence should not be capitalized.

6. *Mr.* (*Messrs.*), *Mrs.* (*Mesdames* or *Mdmes.*), or *Miss* (*Misses*), as appropriate, are used in the absence of other titles of honor or respect, unless the name is followed by abbreviations indicating degrees or the complimentary title *Esquire.*

EXAMPLES:

Mr. John Jones	Miss Mary Jones
Messrs. Jones and Scott	Misses Mary and Anna Jones
The(the) Messrs. Jones	The(the) Misses Jones
Mrs. John Jones	John Jones, Ph.D.
Mesdames Jones and Scott	John Jones, Esquire

7. *Messrs.* is not used with an exact incorporated name or with the name of a firm as given in its letterhead.

EXAMPLES:

Smith & Jones, Inc. (exact incorporated name)
Abel & Carlton (letterhead)
Hall, Johns, and Company (letterhead)
Messrs. may be used in addressing or referring to two or more members of a firm as individuals, such as: Messrs. Smith and Jones.

Below are examples of forms of address, salutation, and complimentary close which follow the general practice of the *U.S. Department of State Correspondence Handbook.*

1. UNITED STATES GOVERNMENT OFFICIALS

The President of the United States

Envelope and Letter Address:	The President or
	The President of the United States
	The White House
	Washington, D.C. (zip code)
Salutation:	The President: (very formal; official)
	Mr. President: (formal)
	My dear Mr. President: (informal)

Complimentary Close:	Respectfully, (formal; official)
	Faithfully yours, (informal; official)
	Very respectfully, (private individuals)

The Vice President of the United States

Envelope and Letter Address:	The Vice President
	United States Senate
	Washington, D.C. (zip code)
Salutation:	Sir: (formal)
	My dear Mr. Vice President: (informal)
Complimentary Close:	Very truly yours, (formal)
	Sincerely yours, (informal)

Note: The Vice President is addressed as *The President of the Senate* in transmitting formal communications, such as reports required by law.

The Chief Justice of the United States Supreme Court

Envelope and Letter Address:	The Chief Justice of the United States
	The Supreme Court of the United States
	Washington, D.C. (zip code)
Salutation:	Sir: (formal)
	My dear Mr. Chief Justice: (informal)
Complimentary Close:	Very truly yours, (formal)
	Sincerely yours, (informal)

Associate Justice of the United States Supreme Court

Envelope and Letter Address:	Mr. Justice (surname)
	The Supreme Court of the United States
	Washington, D.C. (zip code)

Salutation: Sir: (formal)
                                     My dear Mr. Justice: (informal)
Complimentary Close: Very truly yours, (formal)
                                     Sincerely yours, (informal)

Speaker of the House of Representatives

Envelope and Letter Address: The Honorable (full name)
                                Speaker of the House of
                                     Representatives
                                Washington, D.C. (zip code)
Salutation: Sir: (formal)
                                My dear Mr. Speaker: (informal)
Complimentary Close: Very truly yours, (formal)
                                Sincerely yours, (informal)

Under Secretary of a Department

                                (informal only)
Envelope and Letter Address: The Honorable (full name)
                                Under Secretary of State
                                Washington, D.C. (zip code)
Salutation: My dear Mr. (surname):
Complimentary Close: Sincerely yours,

Chief of a Division of a Federal Agency

                                (informal only)
Envelope and Letter Address: Mr. John Doe
                                Chief, Division of Finance
                                Department of State
                                Washington, D.C. (zip code)
Salutation: My dear Mr. Doe:
Complimentary Close: Sincerely yours,

Senator of the United States (man)

Envelope and Letter Address: The Honorable John Doe
                                United States Senate
                                Washington, D.C. (zip code)

Salutation: Sir: (formal)
My dear Senator Doe: (informal)

Complimentary Close: Very truly yours, (formal)
Sincerely yours, (informal)

Note: A woman Senator, of course, is addressed as Madam in the formal salutation. For the House of Representatives, the form is identical except for the second line of the envelope and letter address, which reads instead: House of Representatives. A Representative is addressed as "Mr." Doe or "Mrs." Doe.

Governor of a State

(formal)

Envelope and Letter Address: The Honorable
The Governor of New York
Albany, New York (zip code)

(informal)
The Honorable John Doe
Governor of New York
Albany, New York (zip code)

Salutation: Sir: (formal)
My dear Governor Doe:
    (informal)

Complimentary Close: Very truly yours, (formal)
Sincerely yours, (informal)

Secretary of State (of a State)

Envelope and Letter Address: The Honorable John Doe
Secretary of State of Virginia
Richmond, Virginia (zip code)

Salutation: Sir: (formal)
My dear Mr. Doe: (informal)

Complimentary Close: Very truly yours, (formal)
Sincerely yours, (informal)

Note: Except for the official title, state legislators and mayors are addressed in the same way. The second line, of course, would read instead: "State Legislator" or "Mayor of Buffalo," etc.

2. HEADS OF INDEPENDENT FEDERAL AGENCIES

American National Red Cross

Envelope and Letter Address: The Honorable John Doe
                                President, National Red Cross
                                Washington, D.C. (zip code)
Salutation: Sir: (formal)
                                My dear Mr. Doe: (informal)
Complimentary Close: Very truly yours, (formal)
                                Sincerely yours, (informal)

Note: Except for the official title, other heads of federal agencies are addressed in the same way. The second line, of course, would read: "Chairman, United States Atomic Energy Commission," etc.

3. MEMBERS OF UNITED STATES ARMY, NAVY, AIR FORCE, MARINE CORPS, AND COAST GUARD

Army Officer

Envelope and Letter Address: General of the Army
                                John Doe
                                Department of the Army
                                Washington, D.C. (zip code)
Salutation: Sir: (formal)
                                My dear General Doe: (informal)
Complimentary Close: Very truly yours, (formal)
                                Sincerely yours, (informal)

Navy Officer

Envelope and Letter Address: Admiral John Doe
                                Chief of Naval Operations
                                Department of the Navy
                                Washington, D.C. (zip code)

Salutation:	Sir: (formal)
	My dear Admiral Doe: (informal)
Complimentary Close:	Very truly yours, (formal)
	Sincerely yours, (informal)

Air Force Officer

Envelope and Letter Address:	Lieutenant Colonel John Doe, U.S.A.F.
	Bolling Air Force Base
	Washington, D.C. (zip code)
Salutation:	Sir: (formal)
	My dear Colonel Doe: (informal)
Complimentary Close:	Very truly yours, (formal)
	Sincerely yours, (informal)

Note: The Marine Corps and Coast Guard forms are the same, except for "U.S.M.C.," or U.S.C.G., respectively, instead of U.S.A.F. on the first line of the envelope and letter address.

4. DOCTORS, DEANS, PROFESSORS, LAWYERS AND COURT OFFICERS

President of a University

Envelope and Letter Address:	John Doe, LL.D., Ph.D.
	President,
	George Washington University
	Washington, D.C. (zip code)
Salutation:	Sir: (formal)
	My dear Mr. Doe: (informal)
Complimentary Close:	Very truly yours, (formal)
	Sincerely yours, (informal)
	(Roman Catholic priest)
Envelope and Letter Address:	The Very Reverend
	John Doe, S.J., D.D., Ph.D.
	President, Georgetown University
	Washington, D.C. (zip code)

Salutation: Sir: (formal)
                                     My dear Dr. Doe: (informal)
Complimentary Close: Very truly yours, (formal)
                                     Sincerely yours, (informal)

Dean of a University

                                     (with scholastic degree)
Envelope and Letter Address: John Doe, LL.M., Jur.Sc.D.
                                     Dean, Law Department
                                     Harvard University
                                     Cambridge, Mass. (zip code)
Salutation: ·   Sir: (formal)
                                     My dear Dr. Doe: (informal)
Complimentary Close: Very truly yours, (formal)
                                     Sincerely yours, (informal)

                                     (without scholastic degree)
Envelope and Letter Address: Dean John Doe
                                     Law Department
                                     Harvard University
                                     Cambridge, Mass. (zip code)
Salutation: Sir: (formal)
                                     My dear Dean Doe: (informal)
Complimentary Close: Very truly yours, (formal)
                                     Sincerely yours, (informal)

Professor

                                     (with scholastic degree)
Envelope and Letter Address: John Doe, Ph.D.
                                     Columbia University
                                     New York, New York (zip code)
Salutation: Sir: (formal)
                                     My dear Dr. Doe: (informal)
Complimentary Close: Very truly yours, (formal)
                                     Sincerely yours, (informal)

	(without scholastic degree)
Envelope and Letter Address:	Professor John Doe
	Department of Romance
	Languages
	Columbia University
	New York, New York (zip code)
Salutation:	Sir: (formal)
	My dear Professor Doe:
	(informal)
Complimentary Close:	Very truly yours, (formal)
	Sincerely yours, (informal)

Doctor of Medicine

Envelope and Letter Address:	John Doe, M.D.
	(local address)
Salutation:	Sir: (formal)
	My dear Dr. Doe: (informal)
Complimentary Close:	Very truly yours, (formal)
	Sincerely yours, (informal)

Lawyer

Envelope and Letter Address:	Mr. John Doe
	Attorney at Law
	(local address)
Salutation:	Sir: (formal)
	My dear Mr. Doe: (informal)
Complimentary Close:	Very truly yours, (formal)
	Sincerely yours, (informal)

Presiding Justice

Envelope and Letter Address:	The Honorable John Doe
	Presiding Justice ι
	Appellate Division
	Supreme Court
	New York, New York (zip code)

Salutation: Sir: (formal)
                                         My dear Mr. Justice: (informal)
Complimentary Close: Very truly yours, (formal)
                                         Sincerely yours, (informal)

Judge of a Court
Envelope and Letter Address: The Honorable John Doe
                                         Judge of the United States
                                         District Court of the Southern
                                         District of California
                                         Los Angeles, Calif. (zip code)
Salutation: Sir: (formal)
                                         My dear Judge Doe: (informal)
Complimentary Close: Very truly yours, (formal)
                                         Sincerely yours, (informal)

Clerks of Courts
Envelope and Letter Address: John Doe, Esquire
                                         Clerk of the (court; if a United
                                             States district court, give
                                             district)
                                         (local address)
Salutation: Sir: (formal)
                                         My dear Mr. Doe: (informal)
Complimentary Close: Very truly yours, (formal)
                                         Sincerely yours, (informal)

Chapter 9

AIDS TO BETTER

SECRETARIAL

PERFORMANCE

Perhaps the ability to assume responsibility is the attribute of a secretary which is most highly appreciated by her executive.

Said a vice president of a large corporation: "Now that my secretary handles many of the clerical and administrative tasks that I just don't have the time to perform, I find I am able to concentrate on the more burdensome details."

"Because my duties keep me constantly out of the office," said a busy sales manager, "I need a secretary who can handle things efficiently while I am away."

Today's executive is truly a "man on the go." He may be off on global jet trips, attending conventions, or taking part in client meetings in or out of town. When he is back in the office, he is attending conferences or giving talks at local business luncheons. In this complex business world, the executive finds that as the pressures mount, more and more is demanded of him. A great deal of the pressure can be removed by a secretary who can help him to meet his day's work. Once you have made yourself a competent specialist, you can help your executive to be more effective in his job.

It is essential that you understand the importance of your role as secretary and carry out effectively and efficiently the responsibilities assigned to you. Your executive expects you to keep your work performance at a high level. The secret to top secretarial performance is knowing every phase of your executive's job, and yours. A bad habit is limiting your knowledge to certain duties. The more you know, the better your chances are for new opportunities and increased earnings. Also, the ease with which you perform your assignments reflects your sound secretarial training. You can improve your work performance in a great many ways and become more and more efficient and valuable. The following suggestions will help you to further your ability.

I. HOW TO SIMPLIFY YOUR WORK DAY

The demand for efficient secretaries exists to a greater degree than ever before. In the business office, much of your day is taken up with dictation, transcription, handling incoming and outgoing mail, answering the telephone, keeping track of appointments, and following through on follow-up. Too often precious time is wasted on needless procedures or mistakes that force you to do your work over. For this reason, everything you know about how to do your work better, faster, and with less effort, will free you to become a more successful and valuable secretary.

As a successful secretary you have to be consistently good. You must have superior skills. You must have a clear and intelligent understanding of the rules and principles of sound business practice. Also, you must have the ability to carry out all the various procedures of the average business office, even if they don't *seem* to be very important.

The real trouble with some secretaries is that they work hard enough, yet they accomplish less than they should. There is no reason why you can't improve your performance and become more and more efficient. Here are some time-saving suggestions which can be put to daily use.

PREPARE ENVELOPES (OR LABELS) IN ADVANCE

In most offices, the executive corresponds regularly with certain people and companies. Instead of typing an envelope or label every time you need one, take some time once or twice a month to type up a supply. They will come in handy when you have a last-minute letter or parcel to send out. Also, you can be sure, during emergencies, that this part of your job is already done.

HANDLE INCOMING MAIL EFFICIENTLY AND SPEED UP REPLIES

The method used in handling incoming mail varies according to the size of the company in which you are employed. In large organizations, incoming mail is usually handled by a central mailing department. The mail is opened (if addressed only to the company), sorted, and delivered to the proper persons as soon as possible.

An efficient secretary is expected to be familiar with all the routine practices for handling the incoming mail. If your mail arrives through a central mailing department, it will be delivered to you at scheduled times each day. The first delivery is usually the largest. It is your responsibility, here, too, to assist your executive as much as possible. Prompt and efficient handling of the mail will make his job and your own easier. The following points will insure speedy replies:

1. When you open the mail, be careful that you don't tear the contents with the letter opener or machine.

2. After you have removed the contents, check the envelope for enclosures and clip them to the letters to which they apply.

3. Of course, you will not open mail that is marked "personal" unless your executive specifically requests you to do this.

4. Sort the mail and divide it into two piles: (a) items that your executive must see; (b) items that can be handled by you.

5. Stack the mail in a pile for your executive in the order of importance, with the most urgent items on top.

6. Instead of just putting the mail on your executive's desk, you can go one step further and get material from the files that will aid him in his replies. The material should, in each case, be clipped or placed close to the newly arrived letter.

DATE INCOMING MAIL AS SOON AS IT ARRIVES

It is important to give the mail top priority in your work day. Prompt and efficient handling on your part will insure speedy replies. It is required of some secretaries to stamp a date and time of arrival on all correspondence. However, in some firms this task is done by a machine in the central mailing department. If you open the mail, then you will be in charge of the entire procedure. When the letters arrive at your desk: (1) open them immediately; (2) check for enclosures and clip them to the letters; (3) then stamp the date. (4) If the time of arrival must also be recorded, indicate that too. Instead of using a separate stamp for the date and time of arrival, there are stamps on the market that indicate both simultaneously.

You will be forming a valuable business habit if you make it a practice to date everything. When you receive and read a letter, memorandum, or report, note your initials and the date. You will always know when the matter in question came up— because you have indicated the *exact date*. Such a habit can save your company thousands of dollars in a law suit, especially if the letter concerns a claim against your company.

PUT POSTAGE STAMPS ON ENVELOPES EASIER AND FASTER

A shortcut for stamping envelopes is this: Spread the envelopes on your desk (five across) so that the place for the stamps is visible on each envelope. Line up three rows containing five envelopes in each, making a total of fifteen envelopes to be stamped. Next, roll a strip of stamps in your right hand. Moisten the backs of a few, and working from left to right, press one against the top envelope. As the stamp sticks, hold it in place with your left thumb and tear off the rest of the strip with your right hand. Then, stack the envelopes in each row, and with the palm of your hand, press down on the stamps to make certain they are stuck securely to the envelopes. Repeat this same procedure for larger quantities.

KEEP A WELL-PLANNED STATIONERY DRAWER

A well-organized stationery drawer can save time in typing. In file folders or in compartments in your desk drawer, place the stationery you will use in the order that you would use to make up a carbon pack.

Put letterheads in the *first* file folder or compartment. (If you use two sizes of letterheads, place the one most frequently used first and the other second.)

In the *second* file folder or compartment, place the second sheets.

In the *third* file folder or compartment, place the onion skin paper.

In the *fourth* file folder or compartment, follow with tissue paper. (If different color tissue paper is used, place these in file folders or compartments according to the number and kinds of copies you usually make.)

And in the *fifth* file folder or compartment, place white bond paper.

Note: If carbon sets are used, place these in a file folder or compartment according to frequency of use.

MAINTAIN AN EFFICIENT OFFICE CALENDAR

A desk calendar is a good reminder system for keeping an accurate and thorough record of appointments, meetings, deadlines, etc. Here is how it works:

1. Keep two calendars—a calendar for yourself and one for your executive.

2. Try to get for yourself a calendar pad with 15-minute or

30-minute time divisions so you can record every item accurately.

3. Your executive's calendar should have space for recording all his appointments, including the other person's name, company, and telephone number, and other information which might affect his schedule.

4. As soon as a date is set, enter it on your executive's calendar and also on your own.

5. Your calendar should have notations of all your executive's activities plus your own activities for the day. You can then check it quickly when you have to confirm an appointment, when you are asked about something, or when you are on the telephone.

6. Your calendar should carry items that you generally bring to your executive's attention, with reminders on jobs that must be completed by a certain date.

7. Check your executive's calendar from time to time to see if he may have entered any appointments that he forgot to tell you about.

Save time by placing telephone calls successively

Did you know that you can use the telephone in such a way as to save you time and increase your telephone efficiency? As secretary to a busy executive, a good portion of your work day will be taken up with placing and receiving calls. You can use your telephone to full advantage if you place your telephone calls successively. When you have to make several calls regarding your work, why not gather the information necessary for each call and place them one after the other. Each interruption to make separate calls means time wasted in putting down and picking up a project. Also, you can get your telephone work done more efficiently if you make it a practice to set aside a certain time each day for this chore.

KEEP A HANDY LIST OF NAMES AND TELEPHONE EXTENSIONS YOU CALL FREQUENTLY

Another time saver is to keep a list of numbers you call often. If you have to continually look up numbers of certain people you or your executive often call, you are wasting valuable time. Make a list of their names, telephone numbers and extensions; and then find a convenient place to keep it. A good idea is to use a 4 x 6 inch or a 3 x 5 inch index card and tape it to a pull-out leaf in your desk.

SAVE TIME—SPEED UP YOUR COLLATING

Time can be wasted by using old-fashioned procedures. Get in the habit of using time savers whenever possible. When collating, a valuable time saver is a rubber finger. This gives you a grip on the paper; it avoids slipping and missed pages.

Another helpful tip: As you remove the top sheet of paper from each pile, start with the pile that contains the last page, and place that sheet in your left hand. Then remove the top sheet from the next pile and place that sheet in your left hand. Repeat this procedure until the first page appears on top of the sheets you have in your left hand. By that time you will have finished your chore of collating.

USE A COPYING MACHINE FOR THAT EXTRA COPY AND SAVE TYPING

The most popular office machine today is the copying machine. A copying machine comes in handy especially after you have finished typing a letter or report and you find that you are left with one copy short. Rather than start typing it all over again, you can make that extra copy quickly and easily on a copying machine.

Save retyping—erase neatly

When a mistake is made it should be erased very neatly, leaving no evidence of the erasure. A neatly made correction not only adds to the neat appearance of your typewritten work, but it cuts down on your retyping time. Each time you have to re-do your work you are consuming unnecessary energy. The use of proper erasing tools will make neat erasures. Here is a quick and easy method:

1. Use both a hard eraser and a soft eraser. Work first with the soft eraser to remove the surface of the ink. Then, use the hard eraser to remove the inked impression. Finally, use the soft eraser again, to smooth the surface.

2. Next, lightly rub a piece of chalk over the erased surface to disguise the erasure. Dust it off lightly with a clean brush or with your finger. Then type in the correction.

A Reminder: To avoid strikeovers appearing on the carbons, be sure to correct the carbons as well as the original.

Keep separate notebooks when you work for more than one executive

When you work for more than one man, it is best to keep separate shorthand notebooks. This will save you the embarrassment of getting correspondence mixed up or typing the wrong dictator's name on letters. And when you have to look up a dictated letter, it is easier to go through ten or fifteen pages of shorthand notes belonging to one dictator than to go through twenty or thirty, even fifty, belonging to two or three dictators.

Transcribe your shorthand notes soon after dictation, if possible

It is indeed an accomplishment if you can transcribe your shorthand notes immediately after your executive stops dictating. This isn't always possible, of course. Occasionally it is necessary to put off transcribing your shorthand notes until you have completed the more urgent assignments. But don't let them go any longer than is absolutely necessary. You undoubtedly know from experience how easily and quickly a shorthand outline, particularly if it was hastily made, can be forgotten. Then you either have to take the time to ponder over the outline or go back to your executive, who may have forgotten by this time exactly what he did say.

READ OVER YOUR SHORTHAND NOTES RIGHT AWAY

When you can't transcribe your shorthand notes immediately after dictation you might do the following: As soon as you return to your desk, take a few minutes to read over your notes and insert the necessary notations for proper punctuation, capitalization, and paragraphing. If a shorthand outline may be read in more than one way, read through the entire sentence to be sure of the correct meaning. And if something is not clear and does not sound quite right, check it immediately with your executive while the matter is still fresh in his mind. It is wiser to ask about it and be right than to be inaccurate and have to re-do your work.

GATHER RELATED FILES AND CORRESPONDENCE BEFORE YOU START TRANSCRIPTION

Organization beforehand is the key to better transcription performance. How many times have you had to stop your typing to dig out pertinent data or related correspondence? A systematic approach to your work will speed you through your tasks. To avoid a break in your transcription, make sure you have the necessary files, correspondence, or enclosures before you begin to type. Cutting down on unnecessary motions means more time to get things done.

II. HOW TO TRANSCRIBE YOUR SHORTHAND NOTES

Taking Dictation

Taking dictation is a very important duty which requires prompt and accurate performance. When you are called upon to take dictation, it is only natural that you will be concerned about getting every word down in shorthand outline. If you can get every word, it is indeed an accomplishment. But will you be able to transcribe your shorthand notes accurately so that they will make sense? Taking dictation does not consist of writing shorthand outlines merely for the purpose of proving one's stenographic ability. It involves a great deal more than that. Memory, concentration, careful listening, and comprehension are all fundamental ingredients of shorthand skill.

Observe the following points:

1. Each morning, your shorthand notebook and well sharpened pencils should be ready for immediate use. (If you use a pen, check to see that it is in good writing order.)

2. Before taking dictation, write the date at the top of the page in your shorthand notebook. This is necessary so you can easily look up the date the letter was dictated if you should be unable to locate it in your files.

3. During dictation, take advantage of pauses or interruptions to read back your shorthand notes and insert notations for proper punctuation, capitalization, and paragraphing (if these are left to your better judgment); also, to make a note of any word or phrase you may have failed to write down.

4. At the end of dictation, bring to your executive's attention any items that you think might give you trouble.

5. Be sure you understand the meaning of each letter that is dictated to you. This will help you in reading back your shorthand notes.

6. If you don't understand something, it is much wiser to ask questions about it than to be inaccurate.

TRANSCRIBING YOUR SHORTHAND NOTES

The manner in which you transcribe your shorthand notes is of paramount importance. As already noted, each letter that you type should be accurately typewritten and neatly placed on the sheet of paper. This is essential if your letter is to make a favorable impression on the person receiving it.

Observe carefully the following shorthand transcribing do's and don'ts:

The Do's

1. Apply correct typewriting techniques in your transcription, transcribing rhythmically, smoothly, with continuity.

2. Unless you are thoroughly familiar with the content, read through each dictated letter, or section of the letter at a time, prior to transcription. This will eliminate reading hesitation and will increase rhythm, accuracy and speed in your transcription.

3. Mentally shape up the size of each letter from the number of paragraphs in the letter. This will assist you in setting marginal stops correctly for the proper placement of the letter on your sheet of paper.

4. Make it a point to keep your eyes on the shorthand outlines being transcribed.

5. Look up doubtful spelling of any word before beginning transcription. It will help you to retain a smooth typing continuity if you don't have to stop to look up the spelling during transcription.

6. Proofread your letter and make any necessary corrections before removing it from the typewriter.

7. After you have typed each letter, draw a single line through your shorthand notes. This is important. In this way you can easily distinguish between those letters you have already typed and those letters that have yet to be typed.

8. Keep a rubberband around the finished notes in your notebook so that your place is immediately ready for the next dictation.

The Don'ts

1. Don't look back and forth from your shorthand notes to the typewritten work.

2. Don't start letters of varying lengths at the same marginal settings.

3. Don't start all letters at the same number of spaces from the top of the sheet.

4. Don't use erratic key stroking; look up for line endings, for operation of machine controls, or for numeral and symbol keys. This will create a break in your typing speed.

5. Don't read too far ahead in your shorthand notes when you are transcribing, as it may cause errors such as the transposition of words or letters, or even omission of words and letters.

Every opportunity you get to perform more accurately in your job, even in these small ways, will prove to your executive that you are preparing yourself for greater responsibilities.

III. HOW TO HAVE AN EFFICIENT FILE SYSTEM

The arrangement of the files is another important office requisite. Some secretaries show little concern regarding this segment of their duties. They allow themselves to get bogged down with their filing by letting it pile up. And when they are ready to file, to get the job over with, they do it all at once with considerable haste. As a result, they place letters and important documents in the wrong file folders. Then when they are asked to locate a letter quickly from the files, they easily become upset because they are unable to locate it.

Placing correspondence in the files merely to be forgotten is futile. This method of filing curtails progress in any office. Instead, think of your files as the office "treasure chest." A place where you can store correspondence and information that will become valuable to you at some future date. For instance, when you are asked to locate a certain letter which was written some time ago, you must be able to find it immediately without any trouble.

Because the files hold valuable information, they *must be kept as accurate and as neat as possible.*

WHAT IS FILING?

Filing is simply the storing away of correspondence or information in an orderly manner according to a system that permits any letter or piece of information to be quickly and easily located.

In order to retrieve information easily from the files, you must effect some system or method of filing—a plan, simple enough so that someone besides you will be able to find things. The best and most simplified system to use is the alphabetical system. Names or subjects are filed in alphabetical order. There are two systems of alphabetical filing:

1. One based on the dictionary—(this system is suitable for small lists).

2. The other based on the telephone directory—(this system is better adapted for longer lists). The subjects are listed in alphabetical order under specific categories that also are arranged in an alphabetical sequence.

Use the system of filing best suited to meet the needs and demands of your office.

Besides the alphabetical system, there are three other systems of filing. They are:

1. *Geographic:* This system is used where location is a major factor, or where lists are prepared for mailing. The files are divided into four categories:
   a. by countries
   b. by states
   c. by cities
   d. alphabetically.

2. *Subject:* This system is best set up on the basis of specific topics such as departments, products, names of individuals, or companies.

3. *Numerical:* This system is extensively used in highly tech-

nical work with a chronological basis. Each file, subject or name is given a code number. An alphabetical card system is used to provide the key to the numbers.

Whatever system of filing you use, it is important that you carefully and consistently follow it. The essential qualities of a good filing system are:

a. Its quickness of reference
b. Its accuracy

How To File

A good filing system is of no avail unless the information that you store in your files can be located immediately. An important factor which makes your file system "foolproof" is your ability to remember the exact location of all filed material. It is true that few people start out with an excellent memory. And only those with a photographic mind are able to make mental images of all the things and objects they see. But you can learn how to develop a good memory if you put your power of concentration to work.

When you are filing, free your mind of everything else but filing, and concentrate on what you are doing. Some secretaries seem to think that this is the time to carry on a social conversation with their fellow-workers. Their topics of discussion might range from the theater, pets, travel, dating, etc. As a result, correspondence could easily be misfiled under any such irrelevant categories.

It is obvious, then, that filing cannot be mechanical. If your file system is to function with complete accuracy, you must make every effort to do a thorough job.

Seven simple steps:

1. Place all material in specific subject groups before you begin to file.

2. Staple together all correspondence which belongs together.

3. All stapled material should be in chronological order with the latest date on top.

4. All papers should be dropped fully into the file folders to maintain a neat appearance and to avoid frayed edges.

5. Miscellaneous or General file folders should be established. These folders should contain such material as does not pertain to the specific categories you have already set up. Be sure, however, that this material is filed alphabetically, then chronologically.

6. As the file folders become frayed at the corners or dirty from finger prints, replace them with new folders.

7. Remove all inactive files to the lower drawers in your file cabinet or to a dead storage space, as soon as they cease to be used.

Note: If you consider filing to be a humble job, remember this: The secretary who handles the "humble jobs" most efficiently is the one who rises in status and responsibility. Your attitude regarding your assignments—whatever they may be—reflects your ability to produce "top quality" work.

IV. HOW TO DEVELOP A GOOD MEMORY

Memory is an important function which enables us to remember facts, ideas, names, faces, dates, and appointments.

Some people are gifted by nature with exceptional powers of memory. Others must constantly develop their capacity for remembering.

Today, the secretary with a trained memory is an invaluable asset in the business office. She is essentially hired to take as much burden as possible from her executive and to be a "memory." Not only must she know and understand nearly everything that concerns her job, she must also remember it.

Remembering is a skill like thinking, talking, reading, and typing. With effort and training, you can do all these things. *Memory training* is equally effective. It is simply a matter of acquiring "know-how."

To have a powerful memory, you must first have the desire to have such a memory. The rewards of a trained memory are great. What's more, you can grow continuously as your basic knowledge increases. Training your memory to become quick and alert makes everything much easier to comprehend.

1. A *good memory* will help you to remember addresses and telephone numbers without looking them up every time.

2. A *good memory* will help you to remember errands, important appointments, and telephone conversations.

3. A *good memory* will enable you to take less time to do your work because you can keep important facts in your head.

4. A *good memory* will help you to recall almost instantly pertinent facts about things without consuming valuable time by having to look up information.

5. A *good memory* will help you to think of the right words or facts when you are conversing with others.

6. A *good memory* will help you to remember what you read and hear.

7. A *good memory* will help you to make more friends and acquire greater popularity by remembering people's names whether at business or social gatherings.

8. A *good memory* will help you to conquer fear and any feelings of inferiority. It will give you a sense of security.

9. A *good memory* will help you to win promotions and higher wages.

There is no reason why you should neglect improving your memory. The opportunity is within reach of all those who have a desire to become more proficient and useful. Don't put it off another day. Begin immediately to learn how to develop a powerful memory.

A successful system of thinking and remembering is of extreme value because through conscientious and proper training your efforts can be guided directly toward your goals.

Following is a four-point memory-building plan that will prove helpful in your daily schedule:

1. Select proper cue words and anchor them in your mind.

2. Remember certain facts connected with a person, such as his business, profession, or hobby.

3. Write down immediately everything that needs to be remembered while it is fresh in your mind.

4. Before sleeping, concentrate on something you want to remember in the morning.

You can make your memory more efficient and of more practical value to you if you will learn and use some memory devices. Three of the most common devices are: (a) numbering; (b) classifying (putting items in alphabetical order); (c) visualizing.

A really good memory depends not only on learning all the different methods for remembering, but also on motivation. Effective motivation is just a matter of wanting to remember certain things for certain purposes.

There is no mystery for mastering memory. Just grasp these simple memory principles and apply them spontaneously in your daily business life.

1. Have an *intention to remember.*

2. Have special *interest* in certain subjects.

3. *Select* the most significant things and concentrate on them.

4. Give special *attention* to something you want to remember.

5. *Understand* thoroughly something you want to learn.

V. HOW TO READ BETTER AND FASTER

We all assume that we know how to read. But, are we gaining sufficient knowledge from the material we read?

It is surprising how faulty reading habits of today's average American adult have placed his reading ability below the "comprehension level." Studies indicate that his reading speed is no better than that of the average eighth grader.

To read rapidly and with comprehension is an acquired skill. A slow reader is the product of poor training at an early age; he is *not* necessarily a person of inferior intelligence. But slow and fast readers include individuals with minds of every type; some of average ability; some below average; and some exceptional.

Defective reading *can* hold back even the most intelligent reader. So, don't let bad reading habits hinder your efficiency. Following are the three most common reading handicaps that you should guard against:

1. Eye Fixations. If you watch a person who is reading, you will see that his eyes go in little jumps, with brief pauses between, as they move across each printed line. These brief pauses are called "eye fixations." It is during these pauses that the eye actually reads.

The *fewer* stops your eyes make, the *faster* you will read. Some people have a *wide eye span* which enables them to see more at a glance, make fewer pauses, and read faster.

To find out if you have a wide eye span, try this experiment: As you read a page in a book, count the number of "fixations" your eyes require per line. Or have someone else watch your eyes as you read, and count the number of pauses on each line. If you find you required several pauses, your eye span is *too* restricted.

The solution is to read the page over and over again, until you have reduced the number of eye fixations to a minimum, that is, no more than three.

2. Subvocalizing. A majority of people, when they read, almost invariably tend to "subvocalize" by unconsciously forming words with the lips.

Here is a method that will enable you to determine whether or not you have this tendency:

As you read, place your index finger across your lips. If you notice any movement, however slight, you are subvocalizing. This habit may be cutting your reading speed in half.

Good results can be obtained if you remember to apply the "phrase reading technique."

Example: If you read by phrases/ you are able/ to grasp

ideas quickly/ and retain more facts. /As you read/ be sure/ of course/ that you do not move your lips/ in any way. /You'll be amazed/ how your reading speed will increase/ as you read each line/ on the page.

But if you read one word at a time you tend to lose track of the thought because it takes you longer to read each sentence.

3. Regressing. When you read, if you look back frequently to check up on a word or a group of words you either missed or misunderstood, you are regressing. This is a very common practice and almost everyone, even the most proficient reader, is inclined to do it to some degree. Lack of attention sometimes causes regression, although some people regress by choice or by habit.

Your failure to retain all the important facts only indicates that your comprehension level is probably unsatisfactory. A conscientious reading program, however, will cut down substantially the number of regressions you make.

You'll be amazed how your reading speed will greatly increase if you make a special effort, everytime you read, to eliminate unnecessary regressions. At the same time, your retention of important facts will increase right along with your speed and comprehension.

Concentration, too, plays an important role in your reading program. Below are two suggestions that will help you to further your power of concentration.

1. Learn to visualize what you read by picturing the information in your mind.

2. Train your eyes to pick up images of words, entire phrases, even sentences, at a challenging speed.

Practice is the key to better reading if positive results are to be attained. Through conscientious and intensive training, even the slowest reader can become a fast reader.

Efficient reading has these three essential ingredients:

1. *Perception*—awareness of objects

2. *Comprehension*—capacity for understanding

3. *Vocabulary*—collection of words

The benefits obtained through good reading skills cannot be overestimated.

In your job, where there is a wide need for improved reading facility, your ability to read faster and better is equivalent to "extra hours" in the day to get things done.

VI. HOW TO IMPROVE YOUR CONVERSATION

Conversation plays an important role in your relation to others. People judge you the moment you speak. To some people, conversation can be a precious asset. To others, it can be a great failing. With it you can either gain friends and success—or lose respect and happiness.

A good talker has acquired the art of conversation. He is welcome in any group. When he talks everyone wants to listen to him and join in the conversation. In business, he has an advantage in the struggle for success. Where others fail, he is able to forge ahead.

How about *you?* Haven't you always wanted to be a good conversationalist? . . .

Have you wondered about some assignment that you thought was going to be yours, and instead, it was given to someone else? . . .

Why shouldn't *you* attain the better things in life? You can become more persuasive, more popular, more important, and more successful, if you will just think what the art of conversation can do for you.

What Good Conversation Does For You

1. It helps you to gain confidence in expressing yourself.

2. It helps you to be at ease with anyone, even with someone you have never met before.

3. It helps you to inspire interesting discussions on almost any subject.

4. It helps you to select, with astonishing accuracy, a stranger's interests.

5. It helps you to develop tact—in changing the subject, without offending the other person, and in keeping the conversation rolling.

6. It helps you to develop a more gracious, pleasing personality.

7. It helps you to develop and put into practice your own creative powers.

8. It helps you to make your hobbies sound interesting to everyone.

9. It helps you to have more power to gain business and social success.

10. It helps you to attain the goals you seek.

To do all of these things effectively, you must learn the *secret* of the art of conversation.

Few people bother to learn either how to converse or why we converse.

Conversation has two purposes: (1) It is an expression of your personality. (2) It is a means by which you improve your relations with others.

And the key to good conversation is interest. To talk effectively, you should make your conversation interesting to the other person so that it will attract your listener's interest. Otherwise, you will appear to be boring and dull.

Question 1: "How do I find interesting things to talk about?"

That is simple. People are naturally interested in others and the outside world. So an account of a person's hobbies or experiences is always welcome.

Begin by asking yourself these questions:

1. Do I have any interesting hobbies?

2. Do I have any interesting experiences at school? In college? Vacation? Travels?

3. What interesting subjects have I studied at school? In college?

4. What interesting books and magazines have I read?

5. What interesting opinions do I have?

6. Will my dreams and ambitions be of interest to others?

In addition to tapping your own resources for interesting conversation material, always make an effort to know other people. They, in their turn, will serve as a storehouse of information for all sorts of interesting things to talk about. From them you can learn what they do, what they have read, what they feel, and what they believe.

Question 2: "Once I have plenty of things to talk about, how do I start a conversation?"

To get a conversation going, you can (1) make a challenging statement, (2) appeal to the other person's ego, (3) arouse his curiosity, (4) or appeal to his creative ability.

Below are examples of conversation starters that should lead to lively discussions:

1. "What do you think of the new Paris fashions for the season?"

2. "Which candidate do you think will win the election?"

3. "What did you think of last night's telecast?"

4. Suppose you want to appeal to a person's creative interest. You might say: "I just bought a dress pattern. Shall I make a full skirt or a straight-line sheath?"

5. If the person lives or lived in California, let us say: "Is the weather in California the same as in New York?"

There are many different ways to start a conversation. All you need is *practice*. Once you've learned the best sources for obtaining all sorts of interesting topics that will stimulate conversation with almost everyone, you'll find yourself remembering and developing ideas practically without effort.

Every opportunity you get to converse will be an exciting adventure. In business, or wherever you happen to be, you will constantly be coming in contact with material that can be used in your conversation with people.

If you aspire to be a good conversationalist, resolve right now to take the first step. Begin a self-improvement program this very day. The secretary who possesses conversational skills will know the rewards of a richer, broader life—a better position, greater prestige, more recognition, and wider esteem and rewards.

SUMMING UP

We come now to this important question: Are you ready to make the most out of your secretarial career?

You may be tired of being an "average" secretary. Or, tired of standing still at your job.

Look around the office and compare your ability with that of other secretaries who are holding the best positions with the top executives.

You can justify a better position and attain it if you will make one simple move—DO SOMETHING CONSTRUCTIVE ABOUT YOUR FUTURE.

Now is the time to prepare yourself for better opportunities in your chosen field. Common sense and conscientious hard work are the *keys* to your success.

In concluding, may I leave you with the following thought:

WHAT IS "WORTH"?

A plain bar of iron is worth $5.00.

This same bar of iron, made into horseshoes, is worth $10.50.

If it is made into needles, it is worth $8,235.

If it is turned into balance springs for watches, it becomes worth $250,000.

The same is true of another kind of material—YOU!

Your worth is determined by what you make of yourself.

INDEX